J Constable

NEW CHURCH PRAISE

FULL MUSIC EDITION

THE SAINT ANDREW PRESS
EDINBURGH

First published 1975
by The Saint Andrew Press
121 George Street Edinburgh
on behalf of
The United Reformed Church in England and Wales

ISBN 0 7152 0311 8

A Melody Edition is also available (ISBN 0 7152 0310 X)

First impression May 1975
Second impression September 1975

Musical art-work by G. E. King
92 Maybury Road, Woking, Surrey

Cover design by J. A. Montgomery

Printed in Great Britain
by William Clowes & Sons Ltd.
London, Colchester and Beccles

CONTENTS

FOREWORD

It might have appeared natural that the United Reformed Church should celebrate the achievement of union by producing a new hymn book. The reasons why a Supplement was preferred to a full-size hymn book will be quite clear. In the first place, its production would have taken so long that by the time it appeared the United Reformed Church would be well past the stage of initial celebration. Secondly, a new hymn book was produced for one of our constituent bodies as recently as 1973. Thirdly, it would have been a very expensive business.

But a fourth reason for confining ourselves to a Supplement is more cogent than any of these. It is that at this particular time a Supplement is positively the right kind of book to produce. In this judgment we follow the Methodists, the Baptists, and the Proprietors of Hymns Ancient and Modern who in recent years have brought out Supplements all of which have great distinction and have proved to be exactly what their constituencies needed.

During the past twenty years or so the developments in hymnody, both in words and in music, have been so strenuous and fast-moving that the editors of a full-size hymnal are faced with problems of choice and judgment far more intricate than those which ever faced their predecessors. There is so much new material which appeals to widely differing tastes and interest and which clamours for inclusion that there would be a real danger of a new hymnal's omitting in undue haste much older material simply to make room for the new. Many classics might have been discarded in the zeal to celebrate the contemporary, so that a new generation of hymn singers would be robbed of much that had nourished their fathers. A Supplement, however, means that all that is in the parent book remains available, and that the repertory is simply enriched by a hundred fresh hymns; the only charge for this bonus is the need to provide two hymn books in church instead of one—and in practice other Christian bodies have not found this at all vexatious.

One thing remains to be said. Congregations will enjoy the new book far more, and use it with greater profit, if arrangements can be made for congregational practices, an activity of which some local congregations are still shy. But, with a little planning, it can be done: sometimes briefly within a service at which a new hymn is to be sung; sometimes more extensively on a Sunday or a weekday; and sometimes, very effectively, by congregations gathered in a district or province for a communal introduction to the new material. Such occasions will be all the more valuable if they happen with reasonable regularity.

So we commend *New Church Praise* to the people of the United Reformed Church and to any others who care to use it. It was said in the Preface to *Congregational Praise* that every generation needs its own hymnal. This supplemental book is offered to the present generation in the hope that it will give new vitality and meaning to the parent books which it is designed to augment. May God be pleased to answer the endeavours of the editors in the cheerful, warm-hearted and adventurous singing of our congregations.

ERIK ROUTLEY

PREFACE

New Church Praise has been produced in response to a demand within the United Reformed Church for a supplementary collection of hymns which might be used alongside the parent books (*Revised Church Hymnary*, 1927; *The Church Hymnary: Third Edition*, 1973; *Congregational Praise*, 1951) as a vehicle for worship in the last quarter of the twentieth century. The General Assembly of 1973 appointed a special committee to prepare such a hymnbook supplement. This committee had the benefit of the advice of a number of local churches which had taken part, during the previous two years, in a pilot scheme for trying out new material. Many recent hymns have been included, to strengthen the weaker sections of the present books; but earlier centuries have not been ignored—Bunyan, Herbert and Watts may still enrich our prayers and praises. It is hoped that the resulting, varied, collection may therefore be useful as a supplement to other standard hymnbooks besides those used in the United Reformed Church.

Many tunes here presented will be unfamiliar to users of *The Church Hymnary* or *Congregational Praise*, and where suitable alternative tunes may be recommended a cross-reference is provided. A special feature of this book, however, is the frequent interlining of at least the first verse below the melody, in both the full music and the melody editions, and users are encouraged to take advantage of this provision to add many new tunes to their repertoire.

A further feature of this book is the inclusion of an order of worship for the Lord's Supper (Holy Communion), with specially commissioned musical settings of some of the liturgical material. This order was prepared initially for the United Reformed Church by its Doctrine and Worship Committee, but its blend of the traditional and the contemporary may well commend it to Christians of other denominations.

The Committee offers this collection in the hope that it will make some contribution towards the relevance and vitality of the Church's worship for the coming years.

DEO GLORIA

PETER CUTTS (*Chairman*)
DAVID GARDNER (*Secretary*)

ACKNOWLEDGEMENTS

The compilers wish to thank the following who have given permission for copyright material to be printed. Every effort has been made to trace all copyright owners; but if, through inadvertence, any rights have been overlooked, the necessary correction will gladly be made in subsequent editions. Where no entry is shown in the second column, we have been unable to trace (or make contact with) the owner.

MUSIC

COMPOSER OR ARRANGER	OWNER OR CONTROLLER OF COPYRIGHT	HYMN NO.
Ainslie, J.	Composer	82
Alden, J. H.	Composer	38
Bäck, S.		85
Barrett-Ayres, R.	Stainer & Bell Ltd. (from *Songs for the Seventies*)	2, 8(ii)
Bartlett, L. F..	Composer	80(i)
Blake, L.	Composer	39, 43
Brent Smith A.		15(ii)
Carter, S.	Stainer & Bell Ltd. (from *Songs of Sydney Carter in the Present Tense*)	20
,,	Stainer & Bell Ltd.	41
Cutts, P.	Oxford University Press	1(i), 4, 24(ii), 40, 48(i), 52, 54, 55, 74, 91, 97, 101, 108
Darke, H.	Proprietors of *Hymns Ancient and Modern*	76
Dearnley, C.	Composer	75
Dykes Bower, J.	Proprietors of *Hymns Ancient and Modern*	14
Dyson, G.	Novello and Company Ltd.	92
Evans, D.	Oxford University Press (from *Revised Church Hymnary*)	10 harm., 18 harm.
Gardner, J.	Composer	28
Goodall, D.	British Weekly Ltd.	42
,,	Composer	107
Gooding, Y.	National Christian Education Council 1973	90
Green, J.	Vanguard Music Ltd., 12 Portland Road, London S.E. 25	50
Harris, W. H.	The Executrix for the late Sir William Harris	46, 63
Holst, G.	Roberton Publications (for J. Curwen & Sons Ltd.).	30 (arr.)
Hutchings, A. J. B.	Oxford University Press (from *English Hymnal Service Book*)	17
Jacquet, R. H.	Composer	83, 88
Jagger, A. T. I.	United Reformed Church in England and Wales	19
Langlais, J.	Societé des éditions Philippo, Paris	36
Laycock, G.	Faber Music Ltd., London (from *New Catholic Hymnal*)	71, 84 (arr.)
Llewellyn, W.	Oxford University Press	86
Loring, J. H.	Composer	69
McCarthy, D.	Composer	87
Micklem, T. C.	Composer	3, 6, 8(i), 16, 22, 27, 32, 48(ii), 61, 68, 73, 93(i), 102, 104
Moe, D.	Augsburg Publishing House	58
Murray, A. G.	Composer	29
Newport, D.	Composer	62

Potter, D.	Composer	9
Reid, E.	Stainer & Bell Ltd. (from *New Songs for the Church Book 1*)	23, 100
”	H. C. Reid	31
Routley, E.	from *Eternal Light* (Carl Fischer Inc. Cat. No. 0 4877) © MCMLXXI by Carl Fischer, Inc. New York. International Copyright secured. All rights reserved.	7, 24(i), 94
”	Stainer & Bell Ltd. (from *New Songs for the Church Book 1*)	21
”	Composer	33, 53, 56, 57, 110, 111, 112
Schweizer, R.	© 1966 Hänssler-Verlag, Neuhausen-Stuttgart (from *Bausteine für den Gottesdienst*)	89
Sharpe, E.	Oxford University Press (from *Enlarged Songs of Praise*)	5
Shaw, M.	Oxford University Press (from *Enlarged Songs of Praise*)	72 harm.
”	Oxford University Press (from *Oxford Book of Carols*)	81 harm.
Sheldon, R.	Composer	51 (with descant)
Stanton, W. K.	Oxford University Press (from *B.B.C. Hymn Book*)	37
Stocks, G. G.	The Governors of Repton School	13
Strange, C. E.	Composer	93(ii)
Thiman, E. H.	Composer	80(ii) harm.
Westbrook, F.	The Methodist Church: Division of Education and Youth	47
Williams, D.	Composer	60
Williams, R. Vaughan	Oxford University Press (from *English Hymnal*)	34 arr.
”	Oxford University Press (from *Enlarged Songs of Praise*)	77 arr.
Williams, R. Vaughan (har.) and Broadwood, L. (mel.)	Oxford University Press (from *English Hymnal*)	95
Wilson, J.	Composer	65, 80(i) descants
”	Oxford University Press	98
Wren, B. A.	Oxford University Press	99
Young, C. R.	Harmonisation © 1965: Abingdon Press	1 (ii)
Zimmermann, H. W.	From *Five Hymns* by Heinz Werner Zimmermann, copyright 1973 by Concordia Publishing House. Used by permission.	79

WORDS

AUTHOR OR TRANSLATOR	OWNER OR CONTROLLER OF COPYRIGHT	HYMN NO.
Appleford, P.	Josef Weinberger Ltd., from *27 20th Century Hymns*	46
Arlott, J.	Author	34
Bayly, A. F.	Author	48, 60 (part), 78, 109
Bonhoeffer, D.	S.C.M. Press (‘Christians and Pagans’ in *Letters and Papers from Prison* rev. ed. 1967 Versified by W. H. Farquharson)	63
Bridge, B. E.	Free Church Choir Union	96
Bridges, R.	Oxford University Press (from *The Yattendon Hymnal*)	64
Burkitt, F. C.	Society for Promoting Christian Knowledge	76
Caird, G. B.	Author	67
Carter, S.	Stainer & Bell Ltd. (from *Songs of Sydney Carter in the Present Tense*)	20
”	Stainer & Bell Ltd.	41
Collihole, M.	Stainer & Bell Ltd. (from *New Orbit*)	83
Colvin, T. S.		44
Cropper, M.		45, 95
Dearmer, P.	Oxford University Press (from *Songs of Praise*)	30
”	Oxford University Press (from *Oxford Book of Carols*)	72, 81
Dudley-Smith, T.	Author	92
Dunn, V.	Vanguard Music Ltd., 12, Portland Road, London S.E.25.	50

Author	Copyright holder	Hymn
Ferguson, J.	Stainer & Bell Ltd. (from *Songs for the Seventies*)	2
Fraser, I.	Stainer & Bell Ltd. (from *Songs for the Seventies*)	8
„	Stainer & Bell Ltd. (from *New Songs for the Church Book 1*)	54
Gaunt, A.	John Paul: The Preacher's Press	13, 56
Gaunt, H. C. A.	Author	14, 73
Geyer, J. B.	Stainer & Bell Ltd. (from *New Songs for the Church Book 1*)	23
Gill, D. M.	Author	12
Goodall, D.	British Weekly Ltd.	42
„	Author	108
Green, F. Pratt	Oxford University Press	10, 28, 51, 59, 87, 94, 106
„	© Hänssler-Verlag, Neuhausen-Stuttgart (from *Cantate Domino*, English text)	89
Gregory, J. K.	Author	19, 107
„	Proprietors of *Hymns Ancient and Modern*	37
Hartman, O.		85
Herklots, R. E.	Oxford University Press	25
Herve, M. O.	Mayhew-McCrimmon Ltd.	88
Hewlett, M.	Stainer & Bell Ltd. (from *Contemporary loose leaf Hymn Book*)	75
Hilton, D.	National Christian Education Council. 1973.	90
Hughes, D. W.	Mr. J. R. Hughes	7, 17
Icarus P.	Mayhew-McCrimmon Ltd.	82, 97
Jillson, M.	Author	79
Johnson, R.	Author	36: refrain
Jones, R. G.	Author	32
Kaan, F.	Stainer & Bell Ltd. (from *Songs for the Seventies*)	5, 33, 53
„	Stainer & Bell Ltd (from *Pilgrim Praise*).	70, 71, 77, 80, 91
„	Reproduced by permission of B. Feldman & Co., Ltd. 138–140, Charing Cross Road, London W.C.2.	103
King, G.	Stainer & Bell Ltd. (from *New Orbit*)	105
Luff, A.	Stainer & Bell Ltd. (from *New Songs for the Church Book 2*)	21
Micklem, R. and T. C.	Authors	85
Micklem, T. C.	Author	3, 16, 22, 27, 69, 101, 104
„	H. Freeman & Co. 137/140 Charing Cross Road, London W.C.2.	6
New English Bible	*New English Bible* 2nd edition 1970 by permission of Oxford and Cambridge Univ. Presses	68
O'Neill, J.	Author	62
Orchard, S.	Author	61
Phillips, A.	United Reformed Church in England and Wales	43
Pilcher, C. V.	F. E. V. Pilcher	35
Quinn, J.	Geoffrey Chapman Publishers	29
Reid, E.	H. C. Reid	31
„	Stainer & Bell Ltd. (from *New Songs for the Church Book 1*)	100
Rimaud, D.		36
Routley, E.	Stainer & Bell Ltd. (from *New Songs for the Church Book 1*)	1
„	Author	66
Thompson, C.	Author	11
Wren, B. A.	Oxford University Press	9, 18, 36 (part), 39, 40, 52, 55, 57, 58, 74, 93, 98, 99, 102
„	S.C.M. Press (from *Contemporary Prayers for Public Worship* 1967)	24

We are also grateful to Dame Helen Gardner for her gloss on the words of Hymn No. 15.

HYMNS
(1–109)

and

CANTICLES
(110–112)

1

FIRST TUNE

BIRABUS 87.87.

PETER CUTTS (b. 1937)

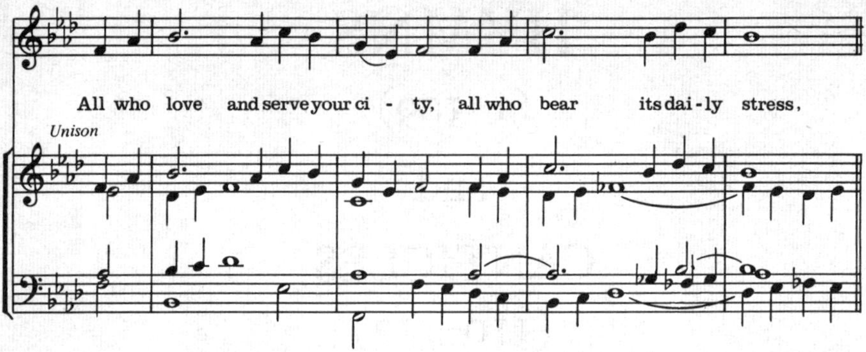
All who love and serve your ci - ty, all who bear its dai - ly stress,
Unison

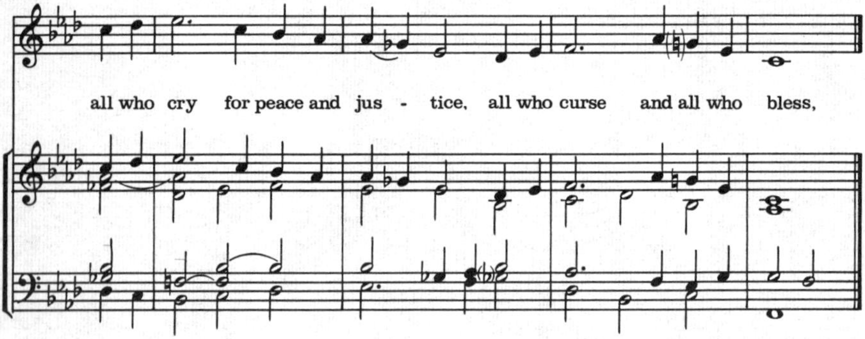
all who cry for peace and jus - tice, all who curse and all who bless,

SECOND TUNE

CHARLESTOWN 87.87.

STEPHEN JENKS'S *American Compiler of Sacred Harmony, No. 1*, 1803.
Harmonised by CARLTON R. YOUNG (b. 1926)

All who love and serve your ci - ty, all who bear its dai - ly stress,
Unison

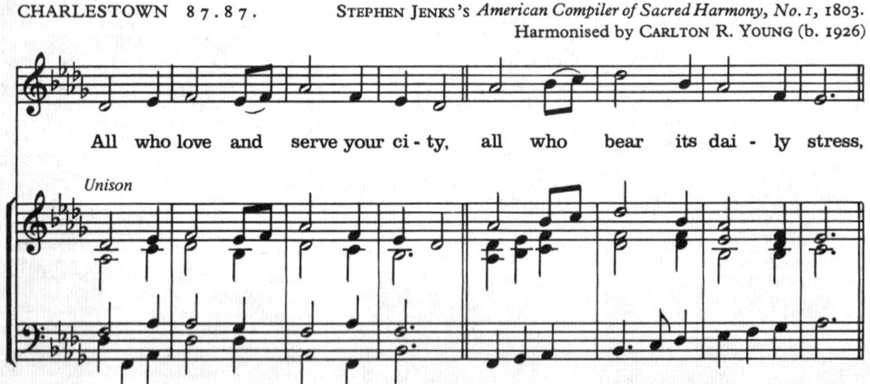

'The Lord is there'

1 All who love and serve your city,
all who bear its daily stress,
all who cry for peace and justice,
all who curse and all who bless,

2 in your day of loss and sorrow,
in your day of helpless strife,
honour, peace and love retreating,
seek the Lord, who is your life.

3 In your day of wealth and plenty,
wasted work and wasted play,
call to mind the word of Jesus,
'Work ye yet while it is day'.

4 For all days are days of judgment,
and the Lord is waiting still,
drawing near to men who spurn him,
offering peace from Calvary's hill.

5 Risen Lord! shall yet the city
be the city of despair?
Come today, our Judge, our Glory;
be its name, 'The Lord is there!'

Erik Routley (b. 1917)

ABEL 76.76.D. REGINALD BARRETT-AYRES (b. 1920)

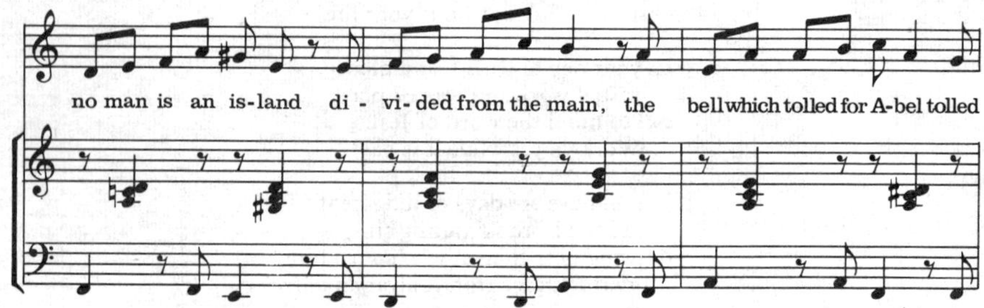

My brother's keeper

1 'Am I my brother's keeper?'—
the muttered cry was drowned
by Abel's life-blood shouting
in silence from the ground.
For no man is an island
divided from the main,
the bell which tolled for Abel
tolled equally for Cain.

2 The ruler called for water
and thought his hands were clean.
Christ counted less than order,
the man than the machine.
The crowd cried, 'Crucify him!',
their malice wouldn't budge,
so Pilate called for water,
and history's his judge.

3 As long as people hunger,
as long as people thirst,
and ignorance and illness
and warfare do their worst,
as long as there's injustice
in any of God's lands,
I am my brother's keeper,
I dare not wash my hands.

John Ferguson (b. 1921)

3

LUMIS — Caryl Micklem (b. 1925)

Caryl Micklem (b. 1925)

This single-verse hymn is meant to be sung (by choir or congregation) as a response to spoken prayer or reading, perhaps repeated several times in the course of a service or of one act of prayer within it. See also 68, 69.

4

BRIDEGROOM 87.87.6. PETER CUTTS (b. 1937)

A and B may be sung by contrasted groups of voices.

Belonging

1 As the bridegroom to his chosen,
as the king unto his realm,
as the keep unto the castle,
as the pilot to the helm,
so, Lord, art thou to me.

2 As the fountain in the garden,
as the candle in the dark,
as the treasure in the coffer,
as the manna in the ark,
so, Lord, art thou to me.

3 As the music at the banquet,
as the stamp unto the seal,
as the medicine to the fainting,
as the wine-cup at the meal,
so, Lord, art thou to me.

4 As the ruby in the setting,
as the honey in the comb,
as the light within the lantern,
as the father in the home,
so, Lord, art thou to me.

5 As the sunshine in the heavens,
as the image in the glass,
as the fruit unto the fig-tree,
as the dew unto the grass,
so, Lord, art thou to me.

Par. from John Tauler (1300–61)
by Emma Frances Bevan (1827–1909)

5

PLATTS LANE 56.64. EVELYN SHARPE (1884–1969) and compilers

As we break the bread and taste the life of wine,

Harmony

we bring to mind our Lord, man of all time.

1 As we break the bread
  and taste the life of wine,
we bring to mind our Lord,
  man of all time.

2 Grain is sown to die;
  it rises from the dead,
becomes through human toil
  our common bread.

3 Pass from hand to hand
  the living love of Christ!
Machine and man provide
  bread for this feast.

4 Jesus binds in one
  our daily life and work;
he is of all mankind
  symbol and mark.

5 Having shared the bread
  that died to rise again,
we rise to serve the world,
  scattered as grain.

Fred Kaan (b. 1929)

6

PADDOCK PLACE 88.88.66

CARYL MICKLEM (b. 1925)
and compilers

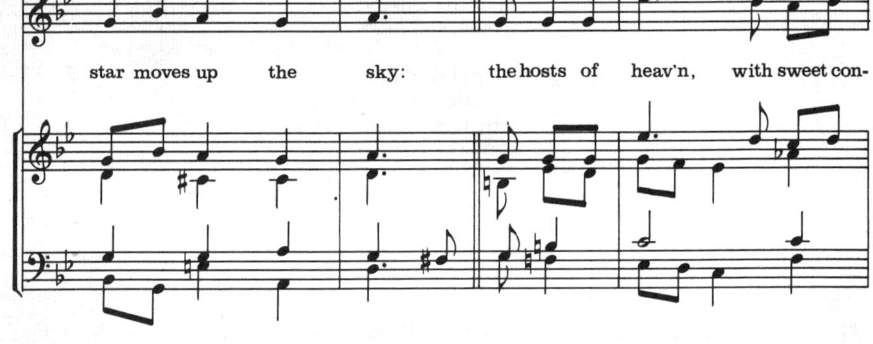

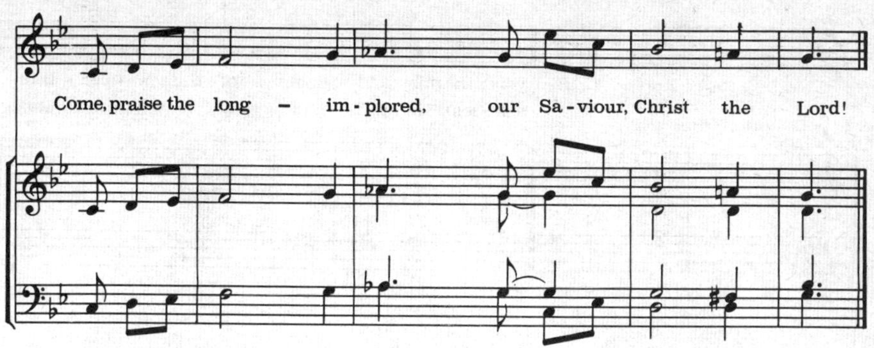

The House of Bread

1 Awake from sleep, the night is spent!
The morning star moves up the sky:
the hosts of heaven, with sweet consent,
proclaim salvation's time is high.
Come, praise the long-implored,
our Saviour, Christ the Lord!

2 While man, the rather sin to choose,
prepares the purple, plants the thorn,
the Word of God our flesh endues
that we, by will of God reborn,
the sons of God may be
to all eternity.

3 Let regal power and humble beast
and shepherd, serving both, attend;
since all, from greatest unto least,
are proffered bliss which shall not end,
where spreads his banquet-board
our Saviour, Christ the Lord.

4 In Bethlehem, the House of Bread,
a richer harvest now is sown;
for none at Jesus' table fed
shall ever thirst or hunger own,
but shall from foes be free
to all eternity.

5 Greet the fulfilment of your dreams,
sad earth, by Adam's plague oppressed!
May he whose lowliness redeems
both north and south, both east and west,
now be by all adored,
our Saviour, Christ the Lord.

Caryl Micklem (b. 1925)

(v. 4) 'Beth-lehem' means in Hebrew 'house of bread'.

7

MAIDEN WAY 66.88.6. ERIK ROUTLEY (b. 1917)

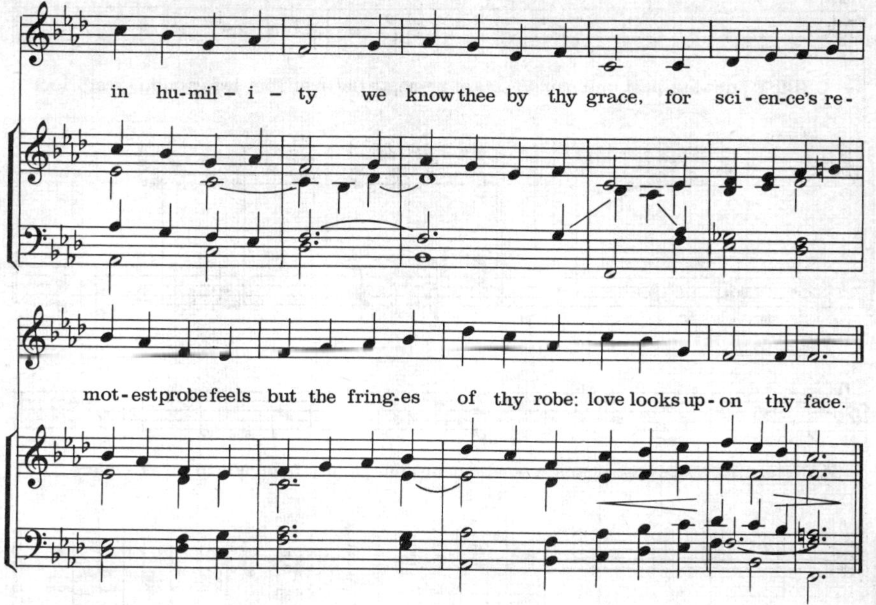

Credo

1 Beyond the mist and doubt
of this uncertain day,
I trust in thine eternal name,
beyond all changes still the same,
and in that name I pray.

2 Our restless intellect
has all things in its shade,
but still to thee my spirit clings,
serene beyond all shaken things,
and I am not afraid.

3 Still in humility
we know thee by thy grace,
for science's remotest probe
feels but the fringes of thy robe:
love looks upon thy face.

Donald Hughes (1911–67)

8

FIRST TUNE

RODEL 655.655 CARYL MICKLEM (b. 1925)

1 CHRIST, burning past all suns,
stars beneath thy feet like leaves on forest floor:
MAN, turning spaceward, shuns
knowledge incomplete, fevered to explore.

2 CHRIST, holding atoms in one
loom of light and power to weave creation's life:
MAN, moulding rocket, gun,
turns creation sour, plots dissolving strife.

3 CHRIST, festive in gay bird,
rush of river flood, joy on lovers' part:
YOUTH, restive, seek new word,
beat of life in blood, chill of death in heart.

4 CHRIST, humble on our side,
snatching death's grim keys, ending Satan's scope:
WE gamble on our guide,
inch our gains of peace, work a work of hope.

Ian Fraser (b. 1917)

The antitheses may be brought out by dividing each verse except the last between two bodies of singers.

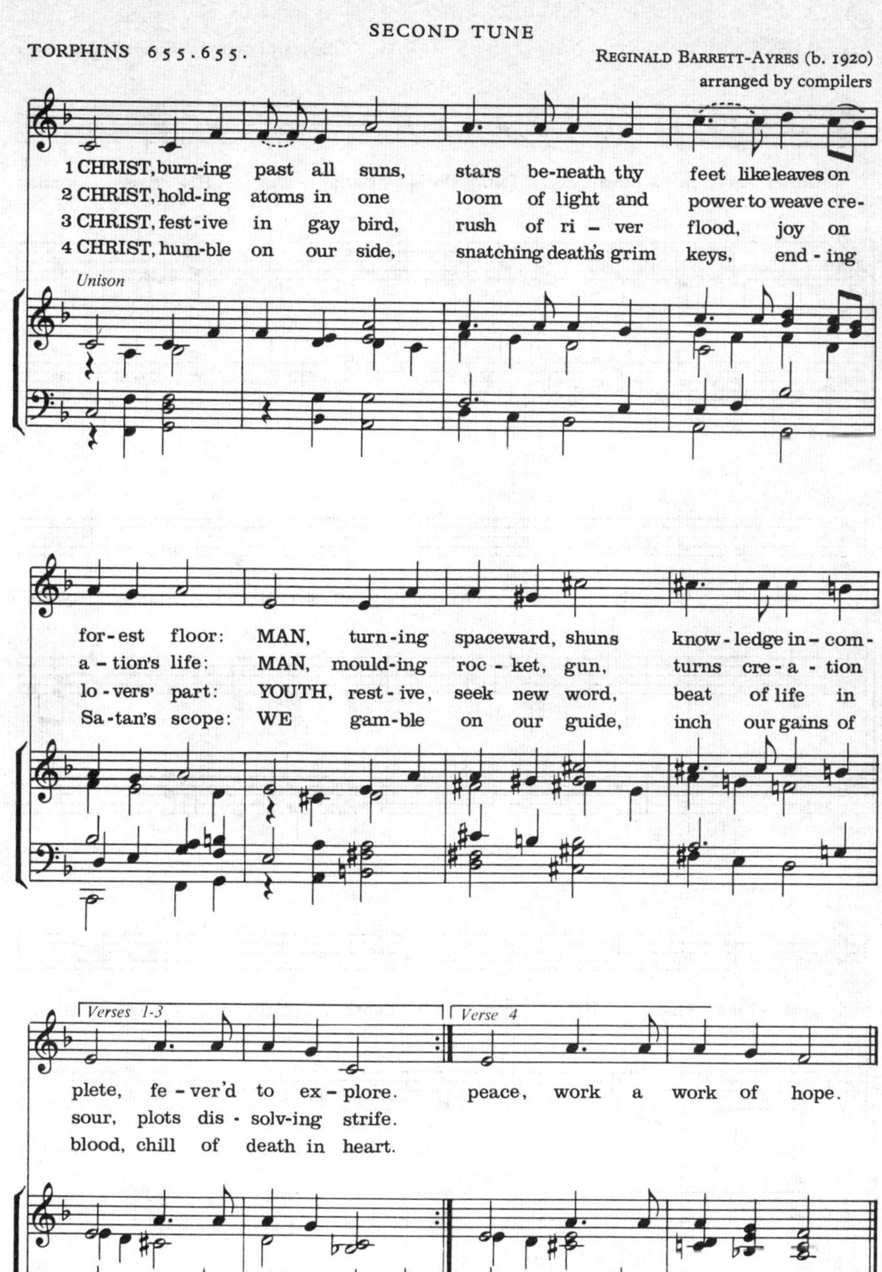
SECOND TUNE
TORPHINS 655.655.
REGINALD BARRETT-AYRES (b. 1920)
arranged by compilers
1 CHRIST, burn-ing past all suns, stars be-neath thy feet like leaves on
2 CHRIST, hold-ing atoms in one loom of light and power to weave cre-
3 CHRIST, fest-ive in gay bird, rush of ri – ver flood, joy on
4 CHRIST, hum-ble on our side, snatching death's grim keys, end - ing
Unison
for-est floor: MAN, turn-ing spaceward, shuns know-ledge in – com-
a – tion's life: MAN, mould-ing roc - ket, gun, turns cre - a - tion
lo - vers' part: YOUTH, rest - ive, seek new word, beat of life in
Sa-tan's scope: WE gam-ble on our guide, inch our gains of
Verses 1-3
Verse 4
plete, fe – ver'd to ex – plore. peace, work a work of hope.
sour, plots dis - solv-ing strife.
blood, chill of death in heart.

9

ST. MARY'S

DOREEN POTTER in *Cantate Domino*, 1974

Alternative tune: TRURO (CH III 446; CP 57; RCH 369; SP 545).

The crucified Lord

1 Christ is alive! Let Christians sing.
His cross stands empty to the sky.
Let streets and homes with praises ring.
His love in death shall never die.

2 Christ is alive! No longer bound
to distant years in Palestine
he comes to claim the here and now
and conquer every place and time.

3 Not throned above, remotely high,
untouched, unmoved by human pains
but daily, in the midst of life,
our Saviour with the Father reigns.

4 In every insult, rift and war
where colour, scorn or wealth divide
he suffers still, yet loves the more,
and lives, though ever crucified.

5 Christ is alive! Ascendant Lord,
he rules the world his Father made
till, in the end, his love adored
shall be to every man displayed.

Brian Wren (b. 1936)

10

CHRISTE SANCTORUM 10 11.11 6.

Melody from *Paris Antiphoner*, 1681
harmonised by DAVID EVANS (1874–1948)

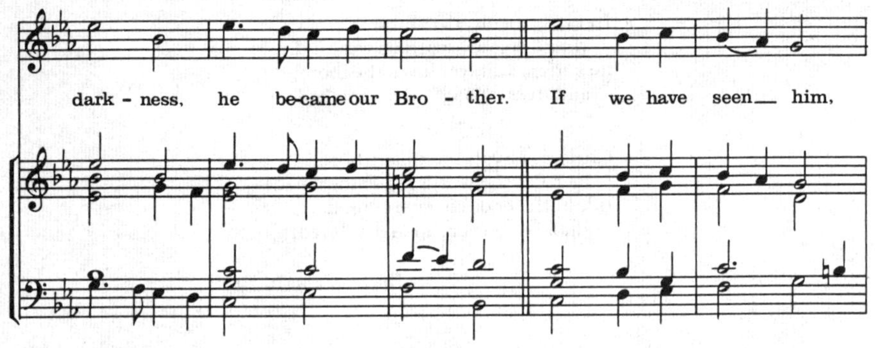

The uniqueness of Christ

1 Christ is the world's Light, he and none other;
born in our darkness, he became our Brother.
If we have seen him, we have seen the Father:
glory to God on high.

2 Christ is the world's Peace, he and none other;
no man can serve him and despise his brother.
Who else unites us, one in God the Father?
glory to God on high.

3 Christ is the world's Life, he and none other;
sold once for silver, murdered here, our Brother—
he, who redeems us, reigns with God the Father:
glory to God on high.

4 Give God the glory, God and none other;
give God the glory, Spirit, Son and Father;
give God the glory, God in man my brother;
glory to God on high.

F. Pratt Green (b. 1903)

11

AVE, VIRGO VIRGINUM

7676.D Trochaic

Melody from Horn's *Gesangbuch*, 1544

At the offering of bread and wine

1 Christian people, raise your song,
chase away all grieving.
Sing your joy and be made strong
our Lord's life receiving.
Nature's gifts of wheat and vine
now are set before us:
as we offer bread and wine
Christ comes to restore us.

2 Come to welcome Christ today,
God's great revelation.
He has pioneered the way
of the new creation.
Greet him, Christ our risen king
gladly recognizing,
as with joy men greet the spring
out of winter rising.

Colin P. Thompson (b. 1945)

12

POLZEATH 11 11 . 11 11 .

English Traditional Carol Melody
arranged by compilers

1 Come, let us remember the joys of the town:
gay vans and bright buses that roar up and down,
shop-windows and playgrounds and swings in the park,
and street-lamps that twinkle in rows after dark.

2 And let us remember the chorus that swells
from hooters and hammers and whistles and bells,
from fierce-panting engines and clear-striking clocks,
and sirens of vessels afloat in the docks.

3 Come, let us now lift up our voices in praise,
and to the Creator a thanksgiving raise,
for towns with their buildings of stone, steel and wood,
for people who love them and work for their good.

4 We thank thee, O God, for the numberless things
and friends and adventures which every day brings.
O may we not rest until all that we see
in towns and in cities is pleasing to thee.

Doris M. Gill
(One verse omitted)

13

SUNSET 98.98.

G. G. STOCKS (1877–1960)

1 Come, living God, when least expected,
when minds are dull and hearts are cold,
through sharpening word and warm affection
revealing truths as yet untold.

2 Break from the tomb in which we hide you
to speak again in startling ways;
break through the words in which we bind you
to resurrect our lifeless praise.

3 Come now, as once you came to Moses
within the bush alive with flame,
or to Elijah on the mountain,
by silence pressing home your claim.

4 So, let our minds be sharp to read you
in sight or sound or printed page,
and let us greet you in our neighbours,
in flaming youth or quiet age.

5 Then, from our gloom, your Son still rising
will thaw the frozen heart of pride
and flash upon us through the shadows
to spread his resurrection wide.

6 And we will share his radiant brightness
and, blazing through the dread of night,
illuminate by love and reason,
for men in darkness, faith's delight.

Alan Gaunt (b. 1935)

14

QUEDGELEY 76.76. Trochaic | JOHN DYKES BOWER (b. 1905)

The gospel

1 Come, Lord, to our souls come down,
   through the gospel speaking;
let your words, your cross and crown,
   lighten all our seeking.

2 Drive out darkness from the heart,
   banish pride and blindness;
plant in every inward part
   truthfulness and kindness.

3 Eyes be open, spirits stirred,
   minds new truth receiving;
make us, Lord, by your own Word,
   more and more believing.

H. C. A. Gaunt (b. 1902)

15

FIRST TUNE

TUNBRIDGE 77.77.

Melody by JEREMIAH CLARKE (c. 1673–1707)

The call

1 Come, my way, my truth, my life:
such a way as gives us breath;
such a truth as ends all strife;
such a life as killeth death.

2 Come, my light, my feast, my strength:
such a light as shows a feast;
such a feast as mends in length;
such a strength as makes his guest.

3 Come, my joy, my love, my heart:
such a joy as none can move;
such a love as none can part;
such a heart as joys in love.

George Herbert (1593–1633)

(v. 2) 'mends in length' means 'grows better as it goes on': cf. *John* 2.10.

15

SECOND TUNE

COME MY WAY 77.77.

A. BRENT SMITH (1899–1950)

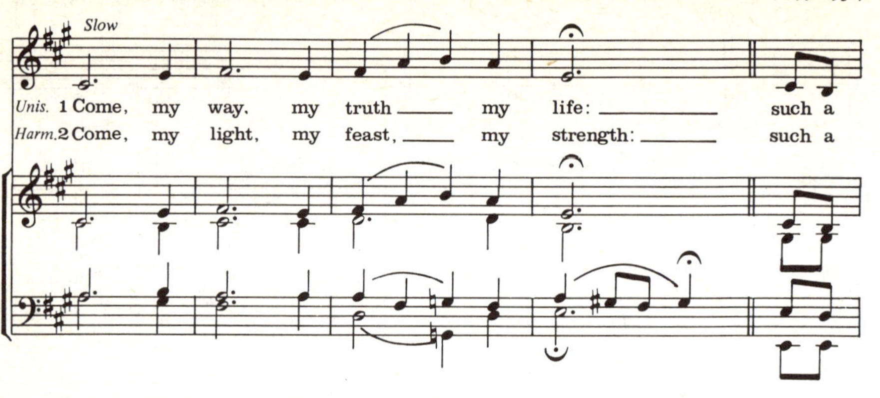

George Herbert (1593–1633)

DOLLIS BROOK

CARYL MICKLEM (b. 1925)

At a wedding

1 Come to our homes to stay,
Lord of this wedding day:
come to us from above
to break the bread of love.
Every good gift that hallows our human life
your mind conceived and shaped.
You and your Church are close as man and wife
or promise made and kept.

2 Father of all, to you
praises and thanks are due:
families everywhere
reflect your loving care.
Make of our lives together a holy thing,
heaven on earth below,
so that to all who meet our love we bring
Christ as the Lord we know.

Caryl Micklem (b. 1925)

17

FUDGIE L. M.

ARTHUR J. B. HUTCHINGS (b. 1906)

Penitence

1 Creator of the earth and skies,
to whom all truth and power belong,
grant us your truth to make us wise;
grant us your power to make us strong.

2 We have not known you: to the skies
our monuments of folly soar,
and all our self-wrought miseries
have made us trust ourselves the more.

3 We have not loved you: far and wide
the wreckage of our hatred spreads,
and evils wrought by human pride
recoil on unrepentant heads.

4 We long to end this worldwide strife:
how shall we follow in your way?
Speak to mankind your words of life,
until our darkness turns to day.

Donald Hughes (1911–67), *altd.*

18

DURROW D. C. M. Irish traditional melody set by DAVID EVANS (1874–1948)

Alternative tune: KINGSFOLD (CH III 212; CP 376; RCH 74; SP 529) using alternative form of lines 5 & 6.

The quest

1 Deep in the shadows of the past,
far out from settled lands,
some nomads travelled with their God
across the desert sands.
The dawn of hope for all mankind
was glimpsed by them alone—
a promise calling them ahead,
a future yet unknown.

2 While others bowed to changeless gods
they met a mystery:
God with an uncompleted name,
'I am what I will be';
and by their tents, around their fires,
in story, song and law
they praised, remembered, handed on
a past that promised more.

3 From Abraham to Nazareth
the promise changed and grew
while some, remembering the past,
recorded what they knew,
and some, in letters or laments,
in prophecy and praise,
recovered, held and re-expressed
new hope for changing days.

4 For all the writings that survived,
for leaders, long ago,
who sifted, chose, and then preserved
the Bible that we know,
give thanks, and find its promise yet
our comfort, strength and call—
the working model for our faith
alive with hope for all.

Brian Wren (b. 1936)

(v. 2) with lines 3 and 4 cf. *Exodus* 3.13 NEB and margin.

19

ST. BAVON 87.87. A. T. I. JAGGER (b. 1911)

Easter morning

1 Early morning. 'Come, prepare him,
   to the tomb your spices bring;
death is cold and death decaying,
   we must beautify our king.'

2 Early morning, women excited,
   seeking Peter everywhere;
telling of a man who told them,
   'He is risen. Don't despair'.

3 Peter racing, early morning,
   to the tomb and rushing in;
seeing shrouds of death dispensed with,
   finding new-born faith begin.

4 Early morning, Mary weeping,
   asking if the gardener knew;
knowing, as his voice says, 'Mary',
   'Lord, Rabbuni, it is you'.

5 'Mary, you can live without me,
   as I now to God ascend;
peace be with you; I am with you
   early morning without end.'

6 Early morning, stay for ever,
   early morning, never cease;
early morning, come to all men
   for their good and power and peace.

John Gregory (b. 1929)

20

EVERY STAR

SYDNEY CARTER (b. 1915)

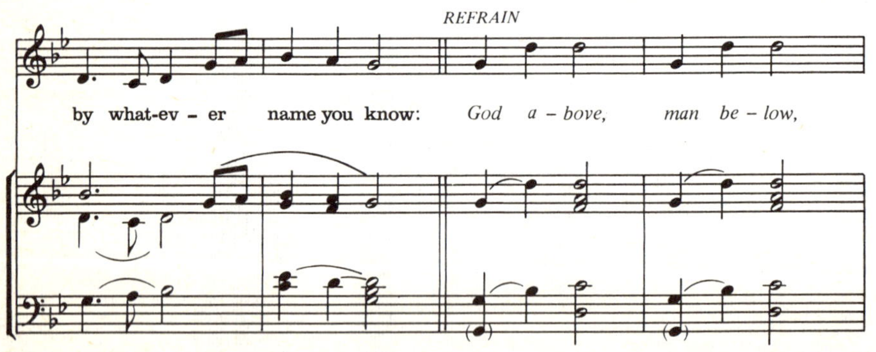

A carol of the universe

1 Every star shall sing a carol;
  every creature, high or low,
come and praise the king of heaven
  by whatever name you know.
God above, man below,
  holy is the name I know.

2 When the king of all creation
  had a cradle on the earth,
holy was the human body,
  holy was the human birth.

3 Who can tell what other cradle,
  high above the Milky Way,
still may rock the king of heaven
  on another Christmas day?

4 Who can count how many crosses,
  still to come or long ago,
crucify the king of heaven?
  Holy is the name I know.

5 Who can tell what other body
  he will hallow for his own?
I will praise the son of Mary,
  brother of my blood and bone.

6 Every star and every planet,
  every creature, high and low,
come and praise the king of heaven
  by whatever name you know.

Sydney Carter (b. 1915)

21

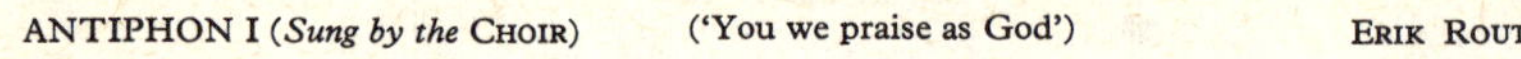

TE DEUM

ANTIPHON I (*Sung by the* CHOIR) ('You we praise as God') ERIK ROUTLEY (b. 1917)

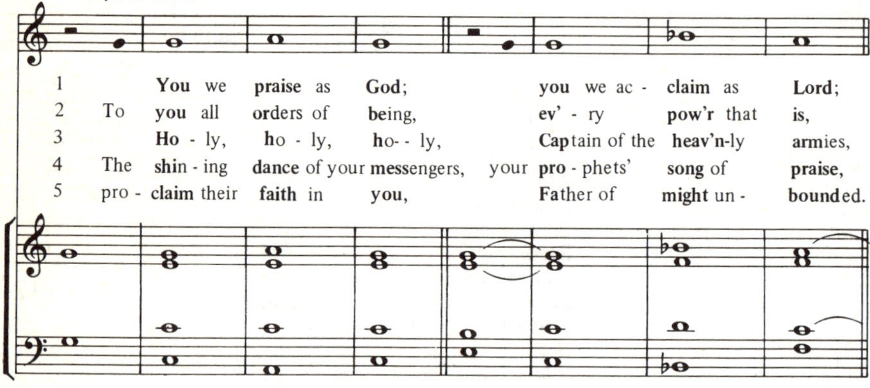

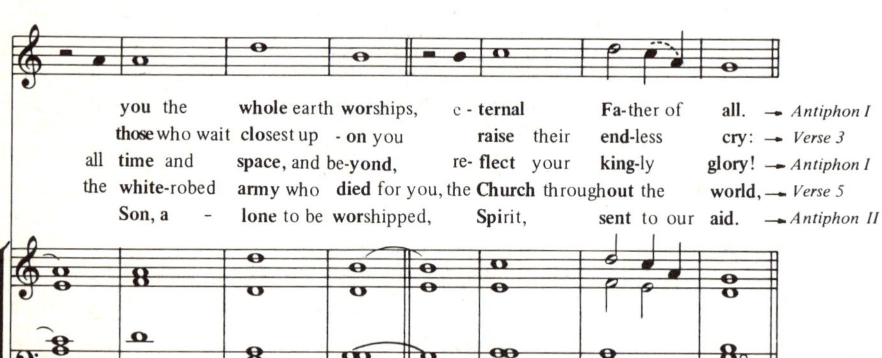

ANTIPHON II *(Sung by the* Choir)

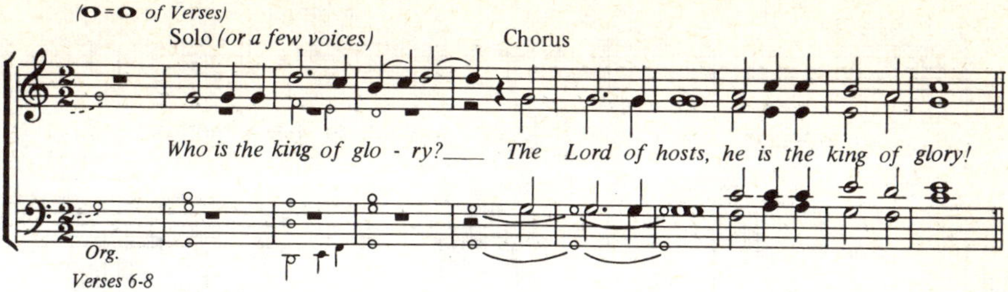
(o = o of Verses)
Solo (or a few voices)
Chorus
Who is the king of glo - ry? The Lord of hosts, he is the king of glory!
Org.

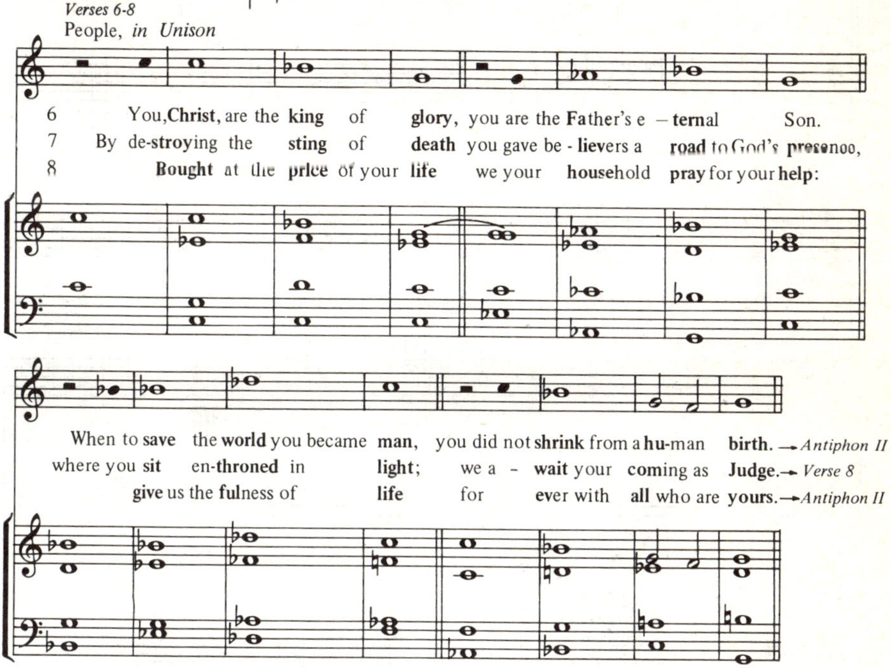
Verses 6-8
People, in Unison
6 You, Christ, are the king of glory, you are the Father's e – ternal Son.
7 By de-stroying the sting of death you gave be - lievers a road to God's presence,
8 Bought at the price of your life we your household pray for your help:
When to save the world you became man, you did not shrink from a hu-man birth. → Antiphon II
where you sit en-throned in light; we a - wait your coming as Judge. → Verse 8
give us the fulness of life for ever with all who are yours. → Antiphon II

AFTER THE LAST ANTIPHON – TO BE SUNG BY ALL:

(o = o of verses)
(Choir in harmony)
AL – LE – LU – IA, AL – LE – LU – IA!

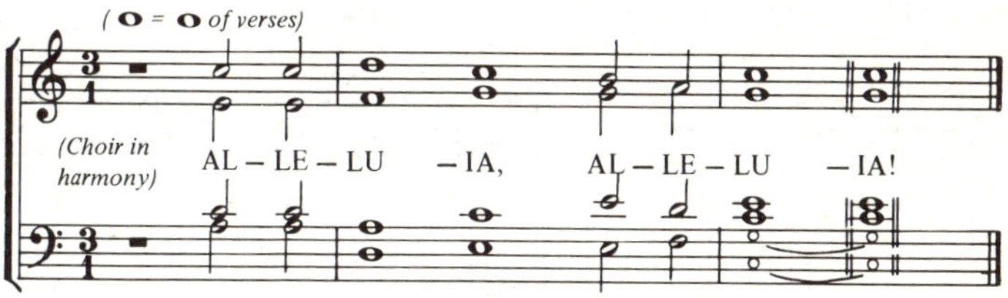

Latin, c.400. Tr. Alan Luff. b.1928

22

ALL KINDS OF LIGHT 5.88.55

CARYL MICKLEM (b. 1925)

All kinds of light

1 Father, we thank you.
For the light that shines all the day;
for the bright sky you have given,
most like your heaven;
Father, we thank you.

2 Father, we thank you.
For the lamps that lighten the way;
for human skill's exploration
of your creation;
Father, we thank you.

3 Father, we thank you.
For the friends who brighten our play;
for your command to call others
sisters and brothers;
Father, we thank you.

4 Father, we thank you.
For your love in Jesus today,
giving us hope for tomorrow
through joy and sorrow;
Father, we thank you.

Caryl Micklem (b. 1925)

23

WESTHOLME

ERIC REID (1936–70)

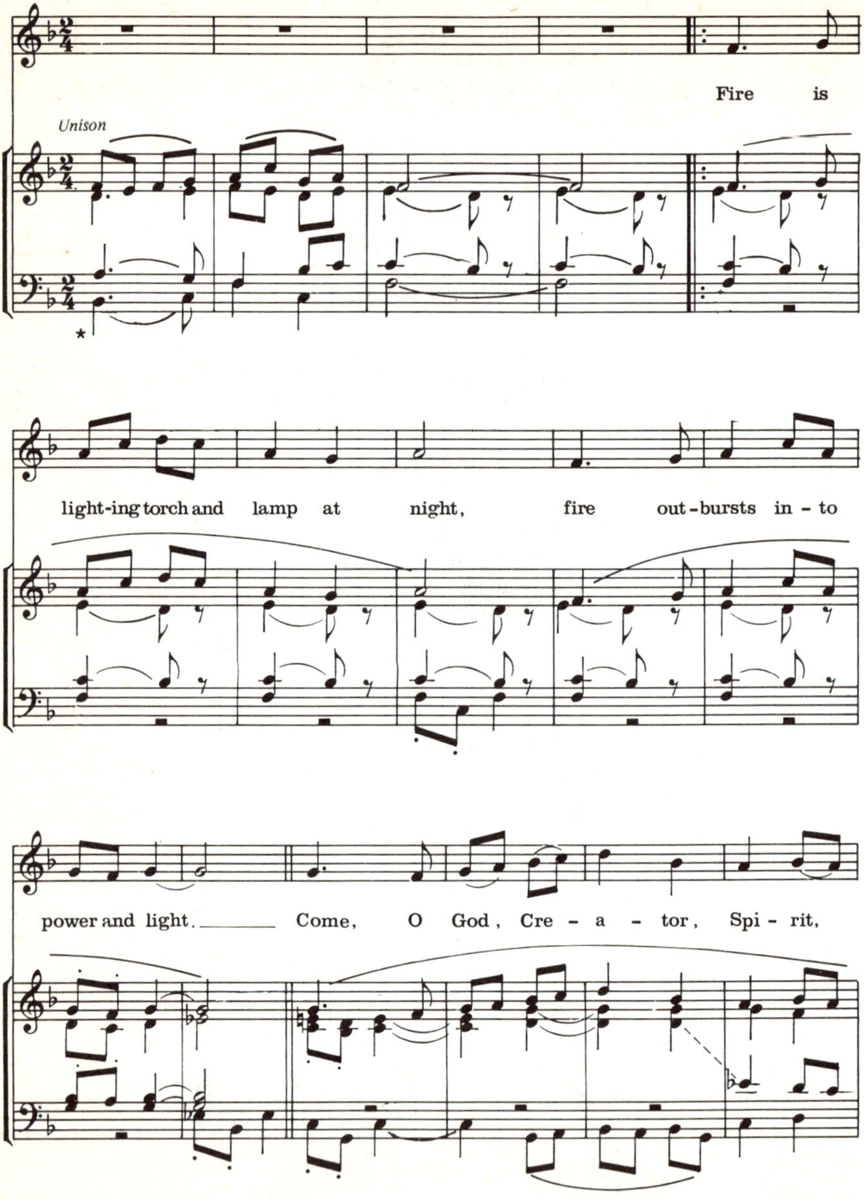
Unison
Fire is
light-ing torch and lamp at night, fire out-bursts in - to
power and light. Come, O God, Cre - a - tor, Spi - rit,

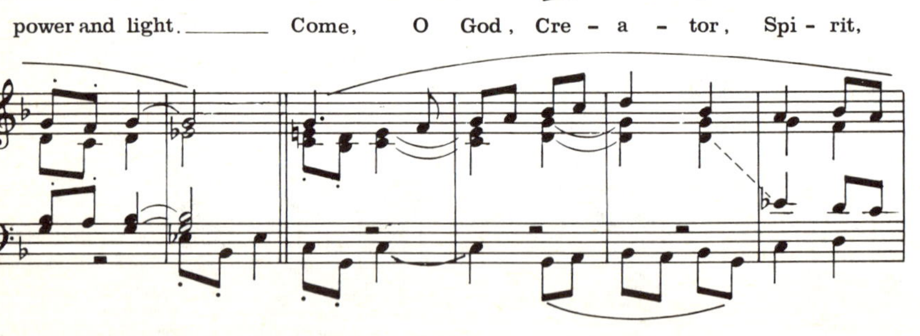

* *Pedal notes for an organ accompaniment are shown by downward stems.*

Creator Spirit

1 Fire is lighting torch and lamp at night,
fire outbursts into power and light.
Come, O God, Creator, Spirit, now,
fill all our lives with your fire.

2 Wind is battering waves of sea on land;
wind is grinding the rocks to sand.
Come, O God, Creator, Spirit, now,
fill all the world with your power.

3 Water gushes down the cleft of space,
living water and spring of grace.
Come, O God, Creator, Spirit, now,
grant us your life and your light.

John B. Geyer (b. 1932), *altd.*

24

FIRST TUNE

THE HAYES 888.84.

ERIK ROUTLEY (b. 1917)

Antiphonal treatment ad lib.

After the Lord's Supper

1 For the bread that we have eaten,
for the wine that we have tasted,
for the life that you have given,
Father, Son and Holy Spirit,
we will praise you.

2 For the life of Christ within us
turning all our fears to freedom,
helping us to live for others,
Father, Son and Holy Spirit,
we will praise you.

3 For the strength of Christ to lead us
in our living and our dying,
in the end, with all your people,
Father, Son and Holy Spirit,
we will praise you.

Brian Wren (b. 1936)

SECOND TUNE

MAYFIELD 888.84. PETER CUTTS (b. 1937)

25

FIRST TUNE

FORGIVE OUR SINS C. M.

American folk-hymn melody from *A Supplement to the Kentucky Harmony* (1820)

SECOND TUNE

HERMON C. M.

Melody, and most of the bass, adapted from
JEREMIAH CLARKE (c. 1673–1707)

As we forgive. . .

1 'Forgive our sins as we forgive'
  you taught us, Lord, to pray,
but you alone can grant us grace
  to live the words we say.

2 How can your pardon reach and bless
  the unforgiving heart
that broods on wrongs and will not let
  old bitterness depart?

3 In blazing light your cross reveals
  the truth we dimly knew,
how small the debts men owe to us,
  how great our debt to you!

4 Lord, cleanse the depths within our souls
  and bid resentment cease;
then, reconciled to God and man,
  our lives will spread your peace.

Rosamond E. Herklots (b. 1905)

26

SING HOSANNA

Traditional, arranged by compilers

1 Give me joy in my heart, keep me praising,
give me joy in my heart, I pray;
give me joy in my heart, keep me praising,
keep me praising till the break of day.
Sing hosanna! Sing hosanna!
Sing hosanna to the king of kings!
Sing hosanna! Sing hosanna!
Sing hosanna to the king!

2 Give me peace in my heart, keep me loving,
give me peace in my heart, I pray;
give me peace in my heart, keep me loving,
keep me loving till the break of day.

3 Give me love in my heart, keep me serving,
give me love in my heart, I pray;
give me love in my heart, keep me serving,
keep me serving till the break of day.

Traditional

GATESCARTH 86.886.

CARYL MICKLEM (b. 1925)
arranged by compilers

Unison

Give to me, Lord, a thankful heart
and a discerning mind:
give, as I play the Christian's part,
the strength to finish what I start
and act on what I find.

1 Give to me, Lord, a thankful heart
and a discerning mind:
give, as I play the Christian's part,
the strength to finish what I start
and act on what I find.

2 When, in the rush of days, my will
is habit-bound and slow
help me to keep in vision still
what love and power and peace can fill
a life that trusts in you.

3 By your divine and urgent claim
and by your human face
kindle our sinking hearts to flame
and as you teach the world your name
let it become your place.

4 Jesus, with all your Church I long
to see your kingdom come:
show me your way of righting wrong
and turning sorrow into song
until you bring me home.

Caryl Micklem (b. 1925)

28

ILFRACOMBE L. M. with Alleluias

JOHN GARDNER (b. 1917)

Alternative tune: TRURO (CH III 498; CP 57; RCH 495; SP 545).

The glorious work of Christ

1 Glorious the day when Christ was born
Alleluia, Alleluia, Alleluia !
to wear the crown that caesars scorn,
Alleluia, Alleluia, Alleluia !
whose life and death that love reveal
Alleluia, Alleluia, Alleluia !
which all men need and need to feel.
Alleluia, Alleluia, Alleluia !

2 Glorious the day when Christ arose,
the surest Friend of all his foes;
who for the sake of those he grieves
transcends the world he never leaves.

3 Glorious the days of gospel grace
when Christ restores the fallen race;
when doubters kneel and waverers stand,
and faith achieves what reason planned.

4 Glorious the day when Christ fulfils
what man rejects yet feebly wills,
when that strong Light puts out the sun
and all is ended, all begun.

F. Pratt Green (b. 1903)

29

UBI CARITAS 13 . 12 12 12 12 — A. Gregory Murray (b. 1905)

REFRAIN

Unison. Not too slow.

VERSES *Harmony ad lib.*

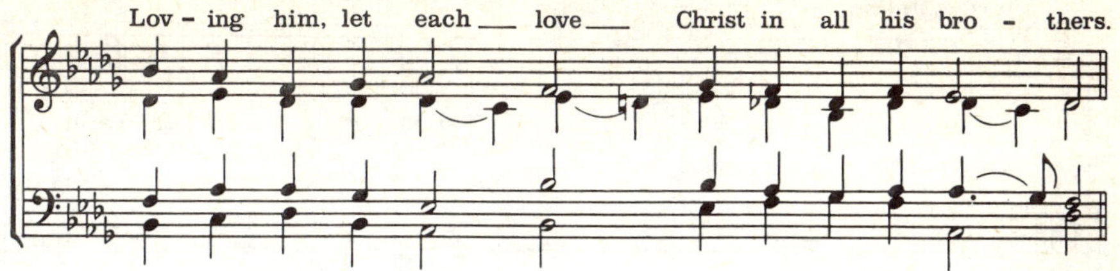

Ubi caritas et amor

REFRAIN
God is love, and where true love is, God himself is there.

1 Here in Christ we gather, love of Christ our calling.
Christ, our love, is with us, gladness be his greeting.
Let us all revere and love him, God eternal.
Loving him, let each love Christ in all his brothers.

God is love, and where true love is, God himself is there.

2 When we Christians gather, members of one Body,
let there be in us no discord, but one spirit.
Banished now be anger, strife and every quarrel.
Christ, our God, be present always here among us.

God is love, and where true love is, God himself is there.

3 Grant us love's fulfilment, joy with all the blessed,
when we see your face, O Saviour, in its glory.
Shine on us, O purest Light of all creation,
be our bliss while endless ages sing your praises.

God is love, and where true love is, God himself is there.

James Quinn, S.J. (b. 1919), *altd.*
(*from the Liturgy of Maundy Thursday*)

30

THEODORIC 666.66.55.3.9.

Melody from *Piae Cantiones*, 1582
arranged by GUSTAV HOLST (1874–1934)

1 God is love: his the care,
tending each, everywhere.
God is love—all is there!
Jesus came to show him,
that mankind might know him.
Sing aloud, loud, loud!
Sing aloud, loud, loud!
God is good! God is truth!
God is beauty! Praise him!

2 None can see God above;
all have here man to love;
thus may we Godward move,
finding him in others,
holding all men brothers.

3 Jesus lived here for men,
strove and died, rose again,
rules our hearts, now as then;
for he came to save us
by the truth he gave us.

4 To our Lord praise we sing—
light and life, friend and king,
coming down love to bring,
pattern for our duty,
showing God in beauty.

Percy Dearmer (1867–1936)

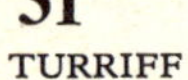

31

TURRIFF

ERIC REID (1936–70)

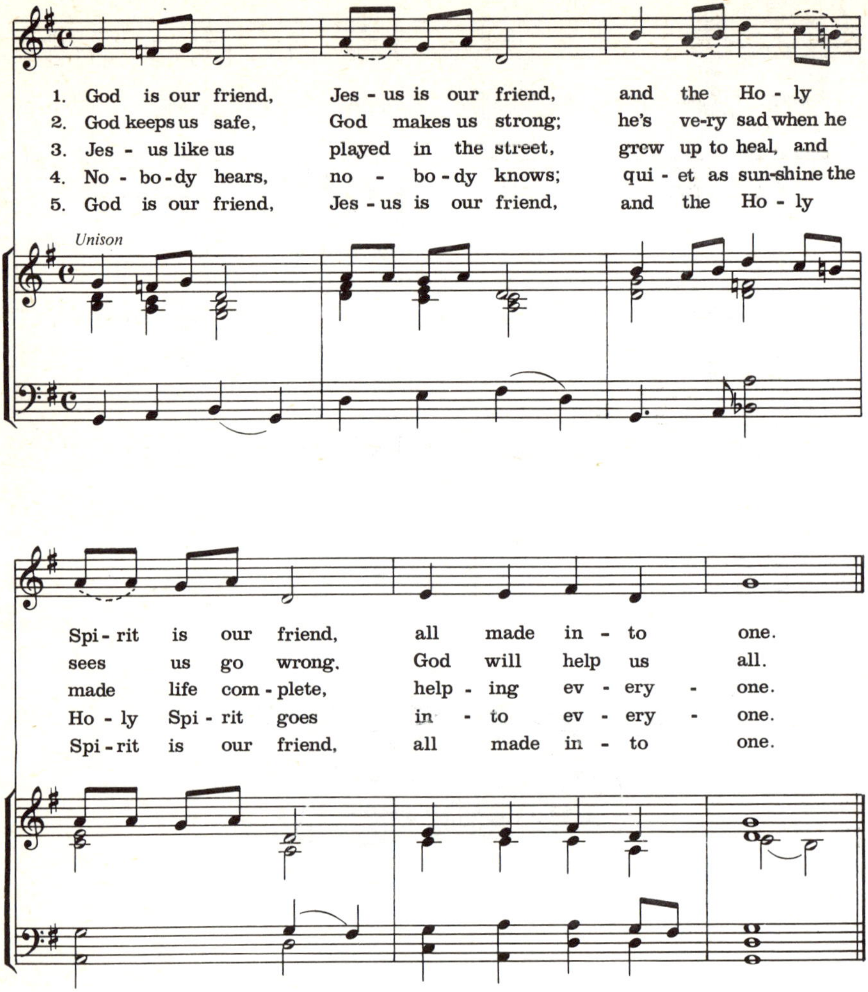

Unison

1. God is our friend, Jesus is our friend, and the Holy Spirit is our friend, all made into one.

2. God keeps us safe, God makes us strong; he's very sad when he sees us go wrong. God will help us all.

3. Jesus like us played in the street, grew up to heal, and made life complete, helping everyone.

4. Nobody hears, nobody knows; quiet as sunshine the Holy Spirit goes into everyone.

5. God is our friend, Jesus is our friend, and the Holy Spirit is our friend, all made into one.

1 God is our friend,
Jesus is our friend,
and the Holy Spirit is our friend,
all made into one.

2 God keeps us safe,
God makes us strong;
he's very sad when he sees us go wrong.
God will help us all.

3 Jesus like us
played in the street,
grew up to heal, and made life complete,
helping everyone.

4 Nobody hears,
nobody knows;
quiet as sunshine the Holy Spirit goes
into everyone.

5 God is our friend,
Jesus is our friend,
and the Holy Spirit is our friend,
all made into one.

Eric Reid (1936–70)

ZEALS 77.77.77

CARYL MICKLEM (b. 1925)

'The earth is the Lord's'

1 God of concrete, God of steel,
God of piston and of wheel,
God of pylon, God of steam,
God of girder and of beam,
God of atom, God of mine,
all the world of power is thine.

2 Lord of cable, Lord of rail,
Lord of motorway and mail,
Lord of rocket, Lord of flight,
Lord of soaring satellite,
Lord of lightning's livid line,
all the world of speed is thine.

3 Lord of science, Lord of art,
God of map and graph and chart,
Lord of physics and research,
word of Bible, faith of Church,
Lord of sequence and design,
all the world of truth is thine.

4 God whose glory fills the earth,
gave the universe its birth,
loosed the Christ with Easter's might,
saves the world from evil's blight,
claims mankind by grace divine,
all the world of love is thine.

Richard G. Jones (b. 1926)

33

CORBRIDGE 87.87.87

ERIK ROUTLEY (b. 1917)

Alternative tune: NEANDER (CH III 313; CP 258; RCH 163; SP 477). The version given in CP needs slight adjustment to accommodate this metre.

The first and final word

1 God who spoke in the beginning,
  forming rock and shaping spar,
set all life and growth in motion,
  earthly world and distant star;
he who calls the earth to order
  is the ground of what we are.

2 God who spoke through men and nations,
  through events long past and gone,
showing still today his purpose,
  speaks supremely through his Son;
he who calls the earth to order
  gives his word and it is done.

3 God whose speech becomes incarnate
  —Christ is servant, Christ is Lord!—
calls us to a life of service,
  heart and will to action stirred;
he who uses man's obedience
  has the first and final word.

Fred Kaan (b. 1929)

34

SUSSEX 8 7 . 8 7 .

Adapted from an English traditional melody
by R. VAUGHAN WILLIAMS (1872–1958)

Alternative tune: SHIPSTON (CH III 17; CP 703; RCH 495; SP 364).

God's farm

1 God, whose farm is all creation,
   take the gratitude we give;
take the finest of our harvest,
   crops we grow that men may live.

2 Take our ploughing, seeding, reaping,
   hopes and fears of sun and rain,
all our thinking, planning, waiting,
   ripened in this fruit and grain.

3 All our labour, all our watching,
   all our calendar of care,
in these crops of your creation,
   take, O God: they are our prayer.

John Arlott (b. 1914)

35

ACH GOTT UND HERR
8 7 8 7 Iambic

Melody from *Andachts Zymbeln*, Freiburg, 1655
arranged by JOHANN SEBASTIAN BACH (1685–1750)

1 Here, Lord, we take the broken bread
  and drink the wine, believing
that by thy life our souls are fed,
  thy parting gifts receiving.

2 As thou hast given, so we would give
  ourselves for others' healing;
as thou hast lived, so we would live,
  the Father's love revealing.

Charles Venn Pilcher (1879–1961)

36

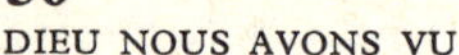

DIEU NOUS AVONS VU

JEAN LANGLAIS (b. 1907)

Organ

(*ff*)

Refrain

God, your glo - ry we have seen in your Son, full of truth, full of heav'nly grace: in Christ make us live, his love shine on our face, and the world will see in us the tri - umph you have won.

Last time.

God, your glory we have seen in your Son,
full of truth, full of heav'nly grace:
in Christ make us live, his love shine on our face,
and the world will see in us the triumph you have won.

1 In the fields of this world his good news he has sown,
and sends us out to reap till the harvest is done.
God, your glory we have seen. . .

2 In his love like a fire that consumes he passed by.
The flame has touched our lips; let us shout, 'Here am I'.
God, your glory we have seen. . .

3 He was broken for us, God-forsaken his cry,
and still the bread he breaks; to ourselves we must die.
God, your glory we have seen. . .

4 He has trampled the grapes of new life on his cross.
Now drink the cup and live; he has filled it for us.
God, your glory we have seen. . .

5 He has founded a kingdom that none shall destroy;
the corner-stone is laid. Go to work: build with joy!
God, your glory we have seen. . .

Didier Rimaud
refrain tr. Ronald Johnson (b. 1913)
verses tr. Brian Wren (b. 1936)

37

HAMBLEDEN 89.89.D. WALTER KENDALL STANTON (b. 1891)

Offertory

1 Good is our God who made this place
whereon our race in plenty liveth.
Great is the praise to him we owe,
that we may show 'tis he that giveth.
Then let who would for daily food
give thanks to God who life preserveth;
offer this board to our good Lord,
and him applaud who praise deserveth.

2 Praise him again whose sovereign will
grants us the skill of daily labour;
whose blessed Son to our great good
fashioned his wood to serve his neighbour.
Shall we who sing not also bring
of this world's wages to the Table?—
giving again of what we gain,
to make it plain God doth enable.

3 So let us our Creator praise,
who all our days our life sustaineth;
offer our work, renew our vow,
adore him now who rightly reigneth;
that we who break this bread, and take
this cup of Christ to our enjoyment,
may so believe, so well receive,
never to leave our Lord's employment.

John Gregory (b. 1929)

38 SHEPHERD BOY'S SONG C. M.

J. H. ALDEN (b. 1900)

Alternative tune: WARWICK (CH III 471; CP 402; RCH 385; SP 513).

1 He that is down needs fear no fall,
he that is low, no pride;
he that is humble ever shall
have God to be his guide.

2 I am content with what I have,
little be it, or much:
and, Lord, contentment still I crave,
because thou savest such.

3 Fulness to such a burden is
that go on pilgrimage:
here little, and hereafter bliss,
is best from age to age.

John Bunyan (1628–88)

This poem, from Part 2 of *The Pilgrim's Progress*, is the Shepherd-Boy's song in the Valley of Humiliation.

39

WINCHCOMBE C. M. LEONARD BLAKE (b. 1907)

Alternative tune: STRACATHRO (CP 182; RCH 451; SP 438) or SONG 67 (CH III 379; CP 435; RCH 433; SP 204).

Christ making friends

1 I come with joy to meet my Lord,
forgiven, loved, and free,
in awe and wonder to recall
his life laid down for me.

2 I come with Christians far and near,
to find, as all are fed,
man's true community of love
in Christ's communion bread.

3 As Christ breaks bread for men to share
each proud division ends.
The love that made us, makes us one,
and strangers now are friends.

4 And thus with joy we meet our Lord.
His presence, always near,
is in such friendship better known:
we see, and praise him here.

5 Together met, together bound,
we'll go our different ways,
and as his people in the world
we'll live and speak his praise.

Brian Wren (b. 1936)

40

SHRUB END 76.76.

PETER CUTTS (b. 1937)

Hope against hope

I Corinthians 1.18–31

1 Here hangs a man discarded,
   a scarecrow hoisted high,
a nonsense pointing nowhere
   to all who hurry by.

2 Can such a clown of sorrows
   still bring a useful word
where faith and love seem phantoms
   and every hope absurd?

3 Can he give help or comfort
   to lives by comfort bound
when drums of dazzling progress
   give strangely hollow sound?

4 Life emptied of all meaning,
   drained out in bleak distress,
can share in broken silence
   my deepest emptiness;

5 and love that freely entered
   the pit of life's despair
can name our hidden darkness
   and suffer with us there.

6 Lord, if you now are risen
   help all who long for light
to hold the hand of promise
   and walk into the night.

Brian Wren (b. 1936)

It is suggested that the first two verses be sung by a soloist or a small group of singers.

41

SHAKER TUNE

Adapted by SYDNEY CARTER (b. 1915)
arranged by JOHN BIRCH (b. 1929)

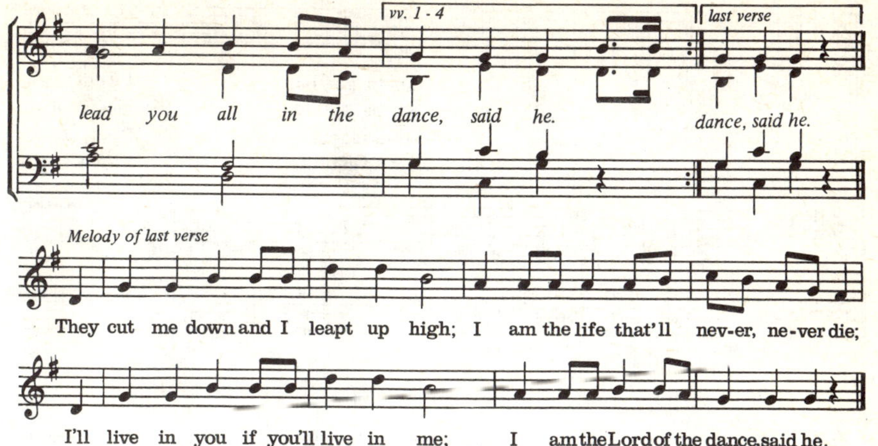

Lord of the dance

1 I danced in the morning when the world was begun,
and I danced in the moon and the stars and the sun,
and I came down from heaven and I danced on the earth;
at Bethlehem I had my birth.
Dance, then, wherever you may be,
I am the Lord of the dance, said he,
and I'll lead you all, wherever you may be,
and I'll lead you all in the dance, said he.

2 I danced for the scribe and the pharisee,
but they would not dance and they wouldn't follow me.
I danced for the fishermen, for James and John—
they came with me and the dance went on.

3 I danced on the Sabbath and I cured the lame;
the holy people said it was a shame.
They whipped and they stripped and they hung me on high,
and they left me there on a cross to die.

4 I danced on a Friday when the sky turned black—
it's hard to dance with the devil on your back.
They buried my body and they thought I'd gone,
but I am the dance, and I still go on.

5 They cut me down and I leapt up high;
I am the life that'll never, never die;
I'll live in you if you'll live in me;
I am the Lord of the dance, said he.

Sydney Carter (b. 1915)

42 SONG FOR A NOT-QUITE-CONVERTED CHRISTIAN

WATERLOO

DAVID GOODALL (b. 1922)

arranged by DONALD SWANN, (b. 1923) and compilers

David Goodall (b. 1922)

43

ACKERGILL 66.66. LEONARD BLAKE (b. 1907)

1 Into a world of dark,
waste and disordered space,
he came, a wind that moved
across the waters' face.

2 The Spirit in the wild
breathed, and a world began.
From shapelessness came form,
from nothingness, a plan.

3 Light in the darkness grew;
land in the water stood;
and space and time became
a beauty that was good.

4 Into a world of doubt,
through doors we closed, he came,
the breath of God in power
like wind and roaring flame.

5 From empty wastes of death
on love's disordered grief
light in the darkness blazed
and kindled new belief.

6 Still, with creative power,
God's Spirit gives to men
a pattern of new life—
and worlds begin again.

Ann Phillips (b. 1930)
and compilers

 CHEREPONI

Melody from N. Ghana, harmonised by compilers

REFRAIN

Jesu, Jesu,
fill us with your love,
show us how to serve
the neighbours we have from you.

1 Kneels at the feet of his friends,
silently washes their feet,
Master who acts as a slave to them.
Jesu, Jesu. . .

2 Neighbours are rich men and poor,
neighbours are black men and white,
neighbours are nearby and far away.
Jesu, Jesu. . .

3 These are the ones we should serve,
these are the ones we should love.
All men are neighbours to us and you.
Jesu, Jesu. . .

4 Kneel at the feet of our friends,
silently washing their feet,
this is the way we should live with you.
Jesu, Jesu. . .

T. S. Colvin, based on a song from N. Ghana

It is suggested that in singing this hymn 'Jesu' should be pronounced 'Yay-soo', as in Greek, Latin, French, German, etc.

45

AU CLAIR DE LA LUNE 11 11 11 11 — Old French melody

1 Jesus' hands were kind hands, doing good to all,
healing pain and sickness, blessing children small,
washing tired feet and saving those who fall.
Jesus' hands were kind hands, doing good to all.

2 Take my hands, Lord Jesus, let them work for you.
Make them strong and gentle, kind in all I do.
Let me watch you, Jesus, till I'm gentle too;
till my hands are kind hands, quick to work for you.

Margaret Cropper (b. 1886)

46

PETERSFIELD 77.77. WILLIAM H. HARRIS (1883–1973)

Christ in us

1 Jesus, humble was your birth
when you came from heaven to earth;
  every day, in all we do,
  make us humble, Lord, like you.

2 Jesus, strong to help and heal,
showing that your love is real;
  every day, in all we do,
  make us strong and kind like you.

3 Jesus, when you were betrayed
still you trusted God and prayed;
  every day, in all we do,
  help us trust and pray like you.

4 Jesus, risen from the dead,
with us always, as you said;
  every day, in all we do,
  help us live and love like you.

Patrick Appleford (b. 1924), *altd.*

The original tune to these words—'Catherine' by Gerard Beaumont C.R.—is to be found in *Twenty-Seven 20th Century Hymns*, published by Josef Weinberger Ltd.

47

YISU NE KAHA

Urdu melody
harmonised by FRANCIS WESTBROOK (b. 1903)

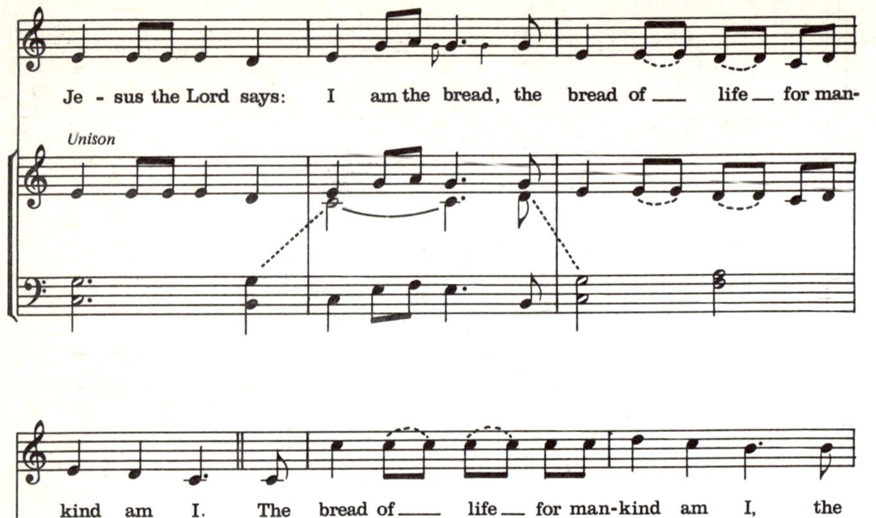

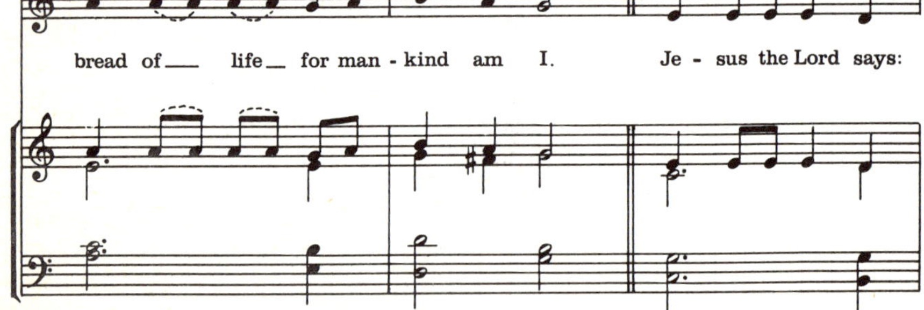

The voice of Jesus

1 Jesus the Lord says, I am the bread,
the bread of life for mankind am I.
  The bread of life for mankind am I,
  the bread of life for mankind am I.
Jesus the Lord says, I am the bread,
the bread of life for mankind am I.

2 Jesus the Lord says, I am the way,
the true and living way am I.

3 Jesus the Lord says, I am the light,
the one true light of the world am I.

4 Jesus the Lord says, I am the shepherd,
the one good shepherd of the sheep am I.

5 Jesus the Lord says, I am the life,
the resurrection and the life am I.

Anonymous,
tr. from the Urdu by Dermott Monahan (1906–57), *altd.*

FIRST TUNE

EMLEY MOOR 6.444.6

PETER CUTTS (b. 1937)

SECOND TUNE

CAERLAVEROCK 6.444.6 CARYL MICKLEM (b. 1925)

1 Joy wings to God our song,
for all life holds
to stir the heart,
to light the mind
and make our spirit strong.

2 Joy wings our grateful hymn,
for home and friends
and all the love
that fills our cup
of gladness to the brim.

3 Joy wings to God our praise,
for wisdom's wealth,
our heritage
from every age,
to guide us in his ways.

4 Joy wings to God our prayer.
All gifts we need
of courage, faith,
forgiveness, peace,
are offered by his care.

5 Joy wings our heart and voice
to give ourselves
to Christ who died
and, risen, lives
that we may all rejoice.

Albert Frederick Bayly (b. 1901)

Two sets of guitar chord symbols are provided as further alternatives to the first and second versions.

SECOND VERSION

KUM BA YAH

1 Kum ba yah, my Lord, kum ba yah!
Kum ba yah, my Lord, kum ba yah!
Kum ba yah, my Lord, kum ba yah!
O Lord, kum ba yah!

2 Someone's crying, Lord, kum ba yah!. . .

3 Someone's singing, Lord, kum ba yah!. . .

4 Someone's praying, Lord, kum ba yah!. . .

Traditional

'Kum ba yah' may be a 'pidgin-English' corruption of 'Come by here'

50

LET THE COSMOS RING

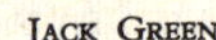

JACK GREEN

REFRAIN

Let the cos - mos ring, ___ as we clap and sing for Je - sus Christ our King. Let the cosmos ring, ___ as we clap and sing for Je - sus Christ our ___ King.

Fine

Valerie Dunn

The verses are best taken antiphonally, the main company singing 'Praise him' (and holding the last note each time), and a leader or group singing 'with the tap of the typewriter' etc. Further verses can be added.

51

JONATHAN 65.65.D.

ROBIN SHELDON (b. 1932)

OPTIONAL DESCANT FOR VERSE 4

Dialogue

1 Life has many rhythms, every heart its beat;
everywhere we hear the sound of dancing feet.
Life is this world's secret: Lord of life, forgive,
if we never asked you what it means to live.

2 *Life is meant for loving*. Lord, if this is true,
why do millions suffer without help from you?
Some who fought injustice added wrong to wrong:
can it be that love is stronger than the strong?

3 It was you who promised: *All who seek shall find.*
What we find lies deeper than our reach of mind;
what we found was you, Lord, you the God above,
you had come, as Victim, to the world you love!

4 *Life is meant for loving*. Lord, if this is true,
love of life and neighbour spring from love of you.
Give us your compassion: yours the name we bear;
yours the only victory we would serve and share.

F. Pratt Green (b. 1903)

52

LITHEROP 87.87.87

PETER CUTTS (b. 1937)

A song of love and living

1 Life is great! So sing about it,
as we can and as we should—
shops and buses, towns and people,
village, farmland, field and wood.
Life is great and life is given.
Life is lovely, free and good.

2 Life is great!—whatever happens,
snow or sunshine, joy or pain,
hardship, grief or disillusion,
suffering that I can't explain—
life is great if someone loves me,
holds my hand and calls my name.

3 Love is great!—the love of lovers,
whispered words and longing eyes;
love that gazes at the cradle
where a child of loving lies;
love that lasts when youth has faded,
bends with age, but never dies.

4 Love is giving and receiving—
boy and girl, or friend with friend.
Love is bearing and forgiving
all the hurts that hate can send.
Love's the greatest way of living,
hoping, trusting to the end.

5 God is great! In Christ he loved us,
as we should, but never can—
love that suffered, hoped and trusted
when disciples turned and ran,
love that broke through death for ever.
Praise that loving, living Man!

Brian Wren (b. 1936)

53

WANSBECK 11.11.11.5 — ERIK ROUTLEY (b. 1917)

Into the world

1 Lord, as we rise to leave this shell of worship,
called to the risk of unprotected living,
willing to be at one with all your people,
we ask for courage.

2 For all the strain with living interwoven,
for the demands each day will make upon us,
and for the love we owe the modern city,
Lord, make us cheerful.

3 Give us an eye for openings to serve you;
make us alert when calm is interrupted,
ready and wise to use the unexpected:
sharpen our insight.

4 Lift from our life the blanket of convention;
give us the nerve to lose our life to others;
be with your church in death and resurrection,
Lord of all ages.

Fred Kaan (b. 1929)

54

RAWTHORPE 6 6.66.88 PETER CUTTS (b. 1937)

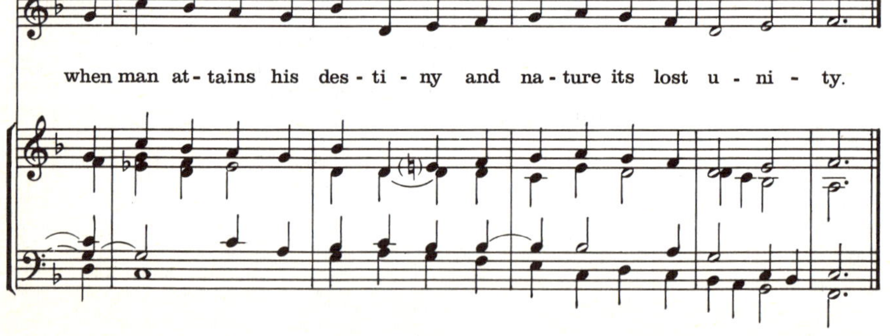

1 Lord, bring the day to pass
when forest, rock and hill,
the beasts, the birds, the grass,
will know your finished will:
when man attains his destiny
and nature its lost unity.

2 Forgive our careless use
of water, ore and soil—
the plenty we abuse
supplied by others' toil:
save us from making self our creed,
turn us towards our brother's need.

3 Give us, when we release
creation's secret powers,
to harness them for peace—
our children's peace and ours:
teach us the art of mastering
which makes life rich and draws death's sting.

4 Creation groans, travails,
futile its present plight,
bound—till the hour it hails
the newfound sons of light
who enter on their true estate.
Come, Lord: new heavens and earth create.

Ian Fraser (b. 1917)

55

HAMPTON POYLE 885.86. PETER CUTTS (b. 1937)

Christian unity

1 Lord Christ, the Father's mighty Son,
whose work upon the cross was done
  all men to receive,
make all our scattered churches one
  that the world may believe.

2 To make us one your prayers were said.
To make us one you broke the bread
  for all to receive.
Its pieces scatter us instead:
  how can others believe?

3 Lord Christ, forgive us, make us new!
What our designs could never do
  your love can achieve.
Our prayers, our work, we bring to you
  that the world may believe.

4 We will not question or refuse
the way you work, the means you choose,
  the pattern you weave,
but reconcile our warring views
  that the world may believe.

Brian Wren (b. 1936)

ABINGDON 88.88.88 ERIK ROUTLEY (b. 1917)

See CP 472 for this tune transposed into C.

1 Lord Christ, we praise your sacrifice,
your life in love so freely given:
for those who took your life away
you prayed, that they might be forgiven;
and there, in helplessness arrayed,
God's power was perfectly displayed.

2 Once helpless in your mother's arms,
dependent on her mercy then,
you made yourself again, by choice,
as helpless in the hands of men;
and, at their mercy crucified,
you claimed your victory and died.

3 Though helpless and rejected then,
you're now as reigning Lord acclaimed;
for ever by your victory
is God's eternal love proclaimed—
the love which goes through death to find
new life and hope for all mankind.

4 So, living Lord, prepare us now
your willing helplessness to share;
to give ourselves in sacrifice
to overcome the world's despair;
in love to give our lives away
and claim your victory today.

Alan Gaunt (b. 1935)

Alternative tune: FOLKINGHAM (CP 573; RCH 637; SP 317).

57

'And can it be...'

1 Lord God, your love has called us here
  as we, by love, for love were made.
Your living likeness still we bear,
  though marred, dishonoured, disobeyed.
We come, with all our heart and mind
your call to hear, your love to find.

2 We come with self-inflicted pains
  of broken trust and chosen wrong,
half-free, half-bound by inner chains,
  by social forces swept along,
by powers and systems close confined
yet seeking hope for all mankind.

3 Lord God, in Christ you call our name
  and then receive us as your own
not through some merit, right or claim
  but by your gracious love alone.
We strain to glimpse your mercy-seat
and find you kneeling at our feet.

4 Then take the towel, and break the bread,
  and humble us, and call us friends.
Suffer and serve till all are fed,
  and show how grandly love intends
to work till all creation sings,
to fill all worlds, to crown all things.

5 Lord God, in Christ you set us free
  your life to live, your joy to share.
Give us your Spirit's liberty
  to turn from guilt and dull despair
and offer all that faith can do
while love is making all things new.

Brian Wren (b. 1936)

Alternative tune: DAVID'S HARP (CP 174; RCH 432; SP 476).

CITY OF GOD 11 10 . 11 10 DANIEL MOE (b. 1924)

Brian Wren (b. 1936)

59

FRANCONIA S. M.

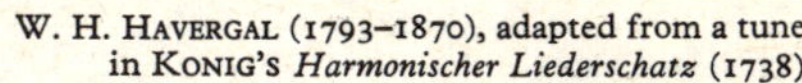

W. H. Havergal (1793–1870), adapted from a tune in Konig's *Harmonischer Liederschatz* (1738) (harmony slightly altered)

Christian baptism

1 Lord Jesus, once a child,
Saviour of young and old,
receive this little child of ours
into your flock and fold.

2 You drank the cup of life,
its bitterness and bliss,
and loved us to the uttermost
for such a child as this.

3 So help us, Lord, to trust,
through this baptismal rite,
not in our own imperfect love,
but in your saving might.

F. Pratt Green (b. 1903), *altd.*

SAN ROCCO C. M. DEREK WILLIAMS (b. 1945)

Alternative tune: LONDON NEW (CH III 6; CP 56; RCH 520; SP 503).

A hymn of the universe

1 Lord of the boundless curves of space
and time's deep mystery,
to your creative might we trace
all nature's energy.

2 Your mind conceived the galaxy,
each atom's secret planned,
and every age of history
your purpose, Lord, has spanned.

3 Your Spirit gave the living cell
its hidden, vital force:
the instincts which all life impel
derive from you, their source.

4 You gave the growing consciousness
that flowered at last in man,
with all his longing to progress,
discover, shape and plan.

5 In Christ the living power of grace
to liberate and lead
lights up the future of our race
with mercy's crowning deed.

6 Lead us, whom love has made and sought,
to find, when planets fall,
that Omega of life and thought
where Christ is all in all.

Albert Frederick Bayly (b. 1901)
and compilers

61

GLENCAPLE 5.6.12 CARYL MICKLEM (b. 1925)

1 Lord, you give to us
the precious gift of life,
a stewardship for every husband, every wife.

2 Lord, you give to us
not only flesh and blood,
but mind and heart and soul to know that they are good.

3 Lord, you offer us
the water, bread and wine.
By faith we reach out for your love within the sign.

4 Lord, you offer us
new life that never ends—
you suffer, serve, and die, and live to call us friends.

5 Lord, you ask of us
a death to what we knew.
Then, rising in your name, we'll put our trust in you.

6 Lord, you share with us
our hope for what will be.
With us prepare each child by love, your love to see.

Stephen Orchard (b. 1942)
and compilers

62 A SONG OF PRAISE FOR ALL THE SAINTS

DOREEN NEWPORT (b. 1927)

Judith O'Neill

63

STONER HILL 10 10 . 10 10 . WILLIAM H. HARRIS (1883–1973)

Alternative tune: SONG 24 (CH III 64; CP 532; RCH 545; SP 103).

1 Men go to God when they are sorely placed,
pray him for succour, for his peace, for bread,
for mercy for them sinning, sick or dead.
All men do so in faith or unbelief.

2 Men go to God when he is sorely placed,
find him poor, scorned, unsheltered, without bread,
whelmed under weight of evil, weak or dead.
Christians stand by God in his hour of grief.

3 God goes to man when he is sorely placed,
body and spirit feeds he with his bread.
For every man, he as a man hangs dead:
forgiven life he gives men through his death.

Dietrich Bonhoeffer (1906–45),
versified by W. H. Farquharson

SONG 20 S. M.

Melody and most of the bass by
ORLANDO GIBBONS (1583–1625)

1 My Lord, my Life, my Love,
to thee, to thee I call:
I cannot live if thou remove;
thou art my joy, my all.

2 My only sun to cheer
the darkness where I dwell;
the best and only true delight
my song hath found to tell.

3 To thee in very heaven
the angels owe their bliss,
to thee the saints, whom thou hast called
where perfect pleasure is.

4 And how shall man, thy child,
without thee happy be,
who hath no comfort nor desire
in all the world but thee?

5 Return, my Love, my Life,
thy grace hath won my heart;
if thou forgive, if thou return,
I will no more depart.

Robert Bridges (1844–1930)
based on a hymn by Isaac Watts (1674–1748)

65

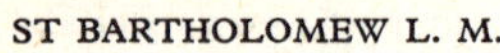
ST BARTHOLOMEW L. M.

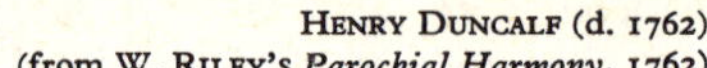
HENRY DUNCALF (d. 1762)
(from W. RILEY'S *Parochial Harmony*, 1762)

Alternative tune: GONFALON ROYAL (CH III 329; CP 169; RCH 23; SP 593), with AMEN after verse 5.

The greatness of God

1 My God, my king, thy various praise
shall fill the remnant of my days;
thy grace employ my humble tongue,
till death and glory raise the song.

2 The wings of every hour shall bear
some thankful tribute to thine ear,
and every setting sun shall see
new works of duty done for thee.

3 Thy truth and justice I'll proclaim;
thy bounty flows, an endless stream;
thy mercy swift; thine anger slow,
but dreadful to the stubborn foe.

4 Let distant times and nations raise
the long succession of thy praise;
and unborn ages make my song
the joy and labour of their tongue.

5 But who can speak thy wondrous deeds?
Thy greatness all our thoughts exceeds;
vast and unsearchable thy ways,
vast and immortal be thy praise.

Isaac Watts (1674–1748),
based on Psalm 145

OPTIONAL DESCANT FOR V.5

arranged by JOHN WILSON

66

GENEVAN PSALM 98 98.98.D.
(RENDEZ A DIEU)

Melody from *La Forme des Prieres et Chants Ecclesiastiques* (Strasbourg, 1545)
(2nd line as in *Genevan Psalter* of 1551)

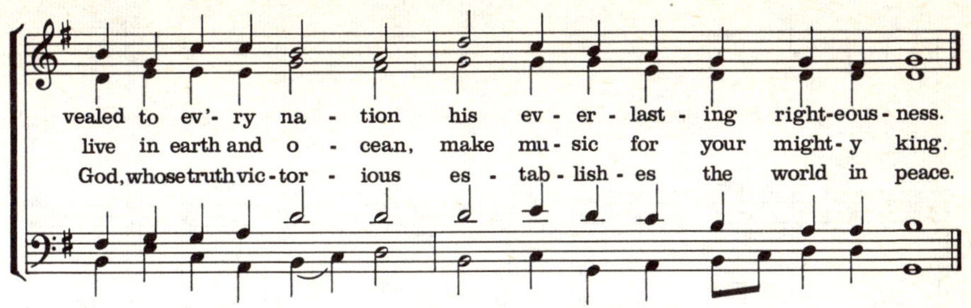

Psalm 98

1 New songs of celebration render
to him who has great wonders done.
Love sits enthroned in ageless splendour:
come and adore the mighty one.
He has made known his great salvation
which all his friends with joy confess:
he has revealed to every nation
his everlasting righteousness.

2 Joyfully, heartily resounding,
let every instrument and voice
peal out the praise of grace abounding,
calling the whole world to rejoice.
Trumpets and organs, set in motion
such sounds as make the heavens ring;
all things that live in earth and ocean,
make music for your mighty king.

3 Rivers and seas and torrents roaring,
honour the Lord with wild acclaim;
mountains and stones look up adoring
and find a voice to praise his name.
Righteous, commanding, ever glorious,
praises be his that never cease:
just is our God, whose truth victorious
establishes the world in peace.

Erik Routley (b. 1917)
tr. from 1970 *revision of the French Psalter*

67

CORNWALL 886.886. S. S. WESLEY (1810–76)

Truth and light

1 Not far beyond the sea, nor high
above the heavens, but very nigh
  thy voice, O God, is heard.
For each new step of faith we take
thou hast more truth and light to break
  forth from thy holy word.

2 Rooted and grounded in thy love,
with saints on earth and saints above
  we join in full accord
to grasp the breadth, length, depth and height,
the crucified and risen might
  of Christ, the incarnate Word.

3 Help us to press toward that mark,
and, though our vision now is dark,
  to live by what we see.
So, when we see thee face to face,
thy truth and light our dwelling-place
  for evermore shall be.

George Bradford Caird (b. 1917)

68

JOHN ONE CARYL MICKLEM (b. 1925)

John 1 . 18, New English Bible

Each of these single-verse hymns is meant to be sung (by choir or congregation) as a response to spoken prayer or reading, perhaps repeated several times in the course of a service or of one act of prayer within it. See also 3.

69

EDMONDSHAM 76.76. JOHN H. LORING (b. 1906)

Par. by CARYL MICKLEM (b. 1925) from *Romans* 8 . 38–9

70

SOLOTHURN L. M. 									Swiss traditional melody

After the Lord's Supper

1 Now let us from this table rise
   renewed in body, mind and soul;
with Christ we die and live again,
   his selfless love has made us whole.

2 With minds alert, upheld by grace,
   to spread the Word in speech and deed,
we follow in the steps of Christ,
   at one with man in hope and need.

3 To fill each human house with love,
   it is the sacrament of care;
the work that Christ began to do
   we humbly pledge ourselves to share.

4 Then grant us courage, father God,
   to choose again the pilgrim way,
and help us to accept with joy
   the challenge of tomorrow's day.

Fred Kaan (b. 1929)

Alternative tune: NIAGARA (CP 58).

71

HARVEST 98.98. (Anapaestic) GEOFFREY LAYCOCK

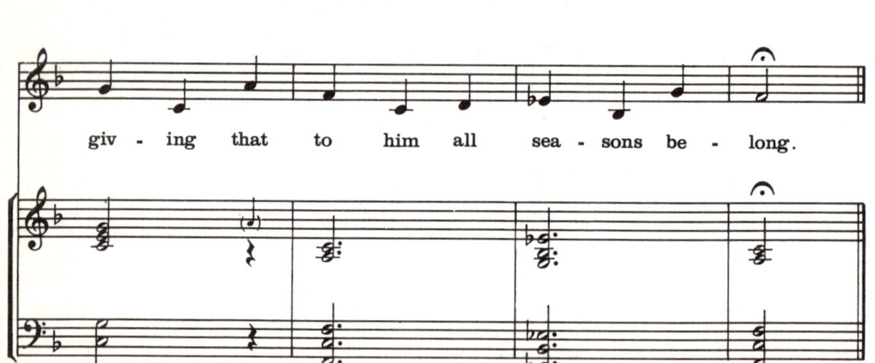

Harvest

1 Now join we, to praise the creator,
   our voices in worship and song;
we stand to recall with thanksgiving
   that to him all seasons belong.

2 We thank you, O God, for your goodness,
   for the joy and abundance of crops,
for food that is stored in our larders,
   for all we can buy in the shops.

3 But also of need and starvation
   we sing with concern and despair—
of skills that are used for destruction,
   of land that is burnt and laid bare.

4 We cry for the plight of the hungry
   while harvests are left on the field,
for orchards neglected and wasting,
   for produce from markets withheld.

5 The song grows in depth and in wideness:
   the earth and its people are one.
There can be no thanks without giving,
   no words without deeds that are done.

6 Then teach us, O Lord of the harvest,
   to be humble in all that we claim;
to share what we have with the nations,
   to care for the world in your name.

Fred Kaan (b. 1929)

72

QUITTEZ, PASTEURS 11.10.11.648.

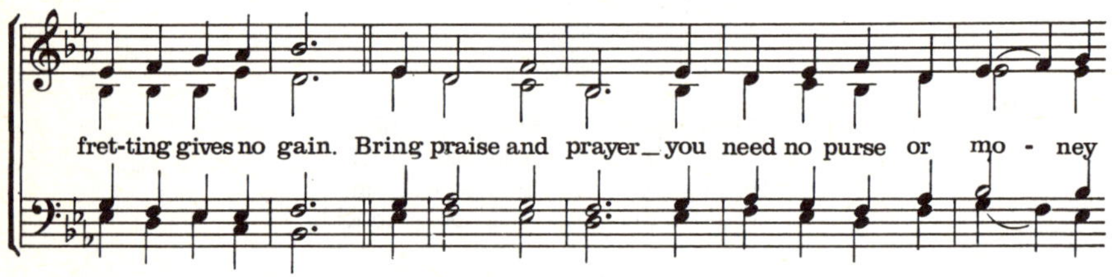

1 Now quit your care,
your anxious fear and worry,
for schemes are vain
and fretting gives no gain.
Bring praise and prayer—
you need no purse or money
for love itself doth cry,
'Come buy, come buy,
come buy, till love shall satisfy'.

2 To bow the head
in sackcloth and in ashes,
or rend the soul,
such grief is not our goal;
but to be led
to where God's glory flashes,
his beauty to come nigh,
to fly, to fly,
to fly where truth and light do lie.

3 For is not this
the fast that I have chosen
(the prophet spoke)
to shatter every yoke,
of wickedness
the grievous bands to loosen,
oppression put to flight,
to fight, to fight,
to fight till every wrong's set right?

4 For righteousness
and peace will show their faces
to those who feed
the hungry in their need,
and wrongs redress,
who build the old waste places,
and in the darkness shine.
Divine, divine,
divine it is when all combine!

5 Then shall your light
break forth as doth the morning;
your health shall spring,
the friends you make shall bring
God's glory bright,
your way through life adorning;
and love shall be the prize.
Arise, arise,
arise! and make a paradise!

Percy Dearmer (1867–1936), *altd.*

The words, based on the carol 'Quittez, Pasteurs', are in part a paraphrase of the Lent lesson, Isaiah lviii. Verses 1 and 2 have been altered by the compilers to make it a hymn for all seasons.

73

WOODMANSTERNE 88.88.88. CARYL MICKLEM (b. 1925)

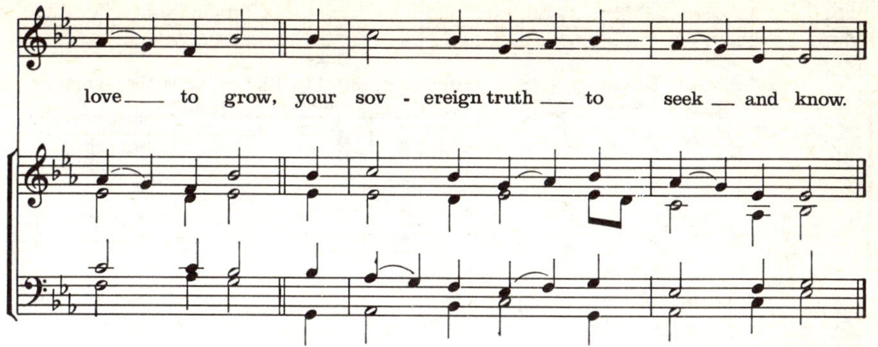

The healing God

1 O God, by whose almighty plan
first order out of chaos stirred,
and life, progressive at your word,
matured through nature up to man;
grant us in light and love to grow,
your sovereign truth to seek and know.

2 O Christ, whose touch unveiled the blind,
whose presence warmed the lonely soul;
your love made broken sinners whole,
your faith cast devils from the mind.
Grant us your faith, your love, your care
to bring to sufferers everywhere.

3 O Holy Spirit, by whose grace
our skills abide, our wisdom grows,
in every healing work disclose
new paths to probe, new thoughts to trace.
Grant us your wisest way to go
in all we think, or speak, or do.

H. C. A. Gaunt (b. 1902)

74

ASKERSWELL D. L. M.

PETER CUTTS (b. 1937)

World Church, World Mission

1 Once from a European shore
men sailed to find and rule the earth,
to purchase slaves with bales of cloth
or take a civilizing law.
Give thanks that some upon that tide,
with faith and failings like our own,
went out to preach in lands unknown
that Christ for every man had died.

2 Give thanks that with the tangled strands
of empire, honour, greed and love
a single world God's Spirit wove
from earth's long-separated lands.
And now that all mankind must face
the dread and hope of being one
give thanks again that Christ is known
in every continent and race.

3 Still in this shrinking world men crave
a nation's glory, might or gain,
and unshared wealth, unheeded pain
divide the master from the slave.
Give thanks that some yet hear the call
and find in Christ a love to span
the bitter chasms made by man
and break each new dividing wall.

4 A great community of hope
by reconciling love reborn
today from all the earth is drawn—
God's pageant and kaleidoscope.
Give thanks that treasures long prepared
—the wisdom, insight, gifts and grace
of every culture, age and place—
in Christ can now be seen and shared.

5 Lord, open out our heart and mind
to glimpse what still the Church could be—
a source of hope and unity,
a prototype for all mankind.
Help us to honour, trust and serve
each unknown friend that Christ has made.
Give us a hope that does not fade,
to build a world of peace and love.

Brian Wren (b. 1936)

75

TRANSFIGURATION 66.85.66.84. CHRISTOPHER DEARNLEY

Flowing smoothly, unhurried

1 Once on a mountain-top
there stood three startled men
who saw the veil of nature drop
and heaven shine in.
Their friend of every day,
the face they knew for his,
they saw for one half-hour the way
he always is.

2 Yet men have lived and died
and found of God no trace.
'Thou art a God' (the prophet cried)
'who hidest thy face.'
The earth lies all explored,
the heavens are ours to climb;
and still no man has seen his God
at any time.

3 And minds that learn to scan
creation like a book
say nothing lives outside their plan
and so never look.
O Lord of hidden light,
forgive us who despise
the things which lie beyond our sight,
and give us eyes.

Michael Hewlett (b. 1916), *altd.*

NAPHILL 7777.D Iambic and Trochaic HAROLD DARKE (b. 1888)

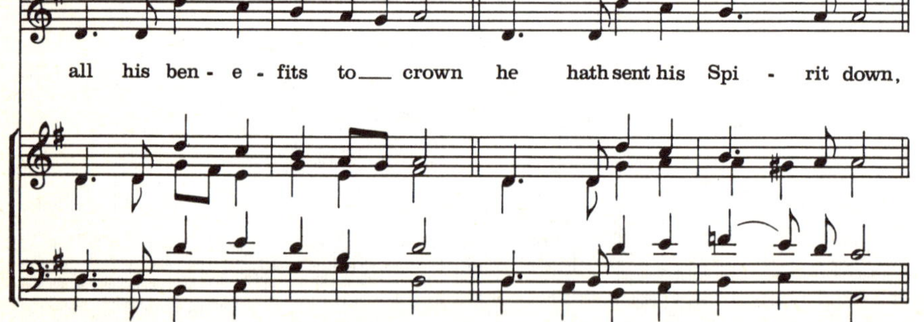

1 Our Lord, his passion ended,
hath gloriously ascended,
yet though from him divided,
he leaves us not unguided;
all his benefits to crown
he hath sent his Spirit down,
burning like a flame of fire
his disciples to inspire.

2 God's Spirit is directing;
no more they sit expecting;
but forth to all the nation
they go with exultation;
that which God in them hath wrought
fills their life and soul and thought,
so their witness now can do
work as great in others too.

3 The centuries go gliding
but still we have abiding
with us that Spirit Holy
to make us brave and lowly—
lowly, for we feel our need,
God alone is strong indeed;
brave, for with the Spirit's aid
we can venture unafraid.

4 O Lord of every nation,
fill us with inspiration!
We know our own unfitness,
yet for thee would bear witness.
By thy Spirit now we raise
to the heavenly Father praise:
Holy Spirit, Father, Son,
make us know thee, ever One.

F. C. Burkitt (1864–1935)

77

OSBORNE C. M.

HENRY CAREY (1692?–1743)
adapted and arranged by R. VAUGHAN WILLIAMS (1872–1958)

Psalm 130

1 Out of our failure to create
a world of love and care;
out of the depths of human life
we cry to God in prayer.

2 Out of the darkness of our time,
of days for ever gone,
our souls are longing for the light,
like watchmen for the dawn.

3 Out of the depths we cry to him
whose will is strong and just;
all human hole-and-corner ways
are by his light exposed.

4 Hope in the Lord whose timeless love
gives laughter where we wept;
the father, who at every point
his word has given and kept.

For verse 3 cf. *John* 3: 19–21.

Fred Kaan (b. 1929)

Alternative tune: NUN DANKET ALL (CH III 252; CP 173; RCH 351; SP 38).

78

BUNESSAN 5 5 5 4. D. Gaelic Melody

1 Praise and thanksgiving,
Father, we offer
for all things living
thou madest good.
Harvest of sown fields,
fruits of the orchard,
hay from the mown fields,
blossom and wood.

2 Bless thou the labour
we bring to serve thee,
that with our neighbour
we may be fed.
Sowing or tilling
we would work with thee;
harvesting, milling,
for daily bread.

3 Father, providing
food for thy children,
thy wisdom guiding
teaches us share
one with another,
so that rejoicing
with us, our brother
may know thy care.

4 Then will thy blessing
reach every people,
all men confessing
thy gracious hand.
Where thy will reigneth
no man will hunger,
thy love sustaineth;
fruitful the land.

Albert Frederick Bayly (b. 1901)

79

LAUDATE PUERI

HEINZ WERNER ZIMMERMANN, (b. 1930)

Small notes in accompaniment for practice only.

Psalm 113

1 Praise the Lord!
Praise, you servants of the Lord,
praise the name of the Lord!
Blessed be the name of the Lord!
Blessed be the name of the Lord
from this time forth and for evermore!
Praise the Lord!
Praise the Lord!

2 Praise the Lord!
Thanks and praises sing to God,
day by day to the Lord!
High above the nations is God.
High above the nations is God,
his glory high over earth and sky.
Praise the Lord!
Praise the Lord!

3 Praise the Lord!
Praise and glory give to God!
Who is like unto him?
Raising up the poor from the dust,
raising up the poor from the dust,
he makes them dwell in his heart and home.
Praise the Lord!
Praise the Lord!

4 Praise the Lord!
Praise, you servants of the Lord,
praise the love of the Lord!
Giving to the homeless a home,
giving to the homeless a home,
he fills their hearts with new hope and joy.
Praise the Lord!
Praise the Lord!

Marjorie Jillson

80

FIRST TUNE

ONE-FIFTY 77.77

LAWRENCE BARTLETT (b. 1933)

SECOND TUNE

ORIENTIS PARTIBUS 77.77 *and Alleluia*

Mediaeval French melody
harmonised by Eric H. Thiman (1900–1975)

Psalm 150

1 Praise the Lord with joyful cry;
let the mood of praise run high.
Praise him who with mighty deeds
human greatness far exceeds.

2 Praise him with the sound that swings,
with percussion, brass and strings.
Let the world at every chance
praise him with a song and dance.

3 Praise with life and voice the Lord,
him who speaks in deed and word,
who to life the world ordained:
let our praise be unrestrained!

Fred Kaan (b. 1929)

When the second tune is used, *Alleluia* may be sung after each verse.

81

RASUMOVSKY

Russian melody, arranged by MARTIN SHAW (1875–1958)

Version [A] may be used throughout if preferred.

1 Praise to God in the highest! Bless us, O Father!
Praise to thee!

2 Guide and prosper the nations, rulers and people:

3 May the truth in its beauty flourish triumphant:

4 May the mills bring us bread, for food and for giving:

5 May the good be obeyed, and evil be conquered:

6 Give us laughter, and set us gaily rejoicing:

7 Peace on earth, and goodwill, be ever amongst us.
Praise to thee!

Russian, tr. Percy Dearmer (1867–1936)

82

WORLEBURY 107.107.46.66 JOHN AINSLIE

1 Reap me the earth as a harvest to God;
gather and bring it again,
all that is his, to the Maker of all:
lift it and offer it high!
Bring bread, bring wine, give glory to the Lord.
Whose is the earth but God's?
Whose is the praise but his?

2 Go with your song and your music, with joy
go to the altar of God.
Carry your offerings, fruits of the earth,
work of your labouring hands.

3 Gladness and pity and passion and pain
—all that is mortal in man—
lay all before him, return him his gift—
God, to whom all shall go home.

'*Peter Icarus*'

83

CHESHUNT

RICHARD H. JACQUET (b. 1947)

1 Ring a bell for peace,
for the babe born on this night,
ring a bell through the country and the town;
ring a bell for peace,
come and see the wondrous light,
ring a bell, ring it merry up and down.

2 Blow a horn for joy,
for the babe born in the hay,
blow a horn through the country and the town;
blow a horn for joy,
come and hear what people say,
blow a horn, blow it merry up and down.

3 Play a flute for hope,
for the babe now fast asleep,
play a flute through the country and the town;
play a flute for hope,
see the shepherds leave their sheep,
play a flute, play it merry up and down.

4 Beat the drum for faith,
for the babe born 'neath the star,
beat the drum through the country and the town;
beat the drum for faith,
come and play where'er you are,
beat the drum, beat it merry up and down.

Marian Collihole

84

SEE THE BABY (AMEN)

Negro Spiritual
arranged by GEOFFREY LAYCOCK

(Amen, amen, amen. . .)

1 See the baby
lying in a manger
on that Christmas morning.

2 See him in the temple
teacher of the teachers
marv'lling at his wisdom.

3 See him at the seaside
healing and proclaiming
to the strong and feeble.

4 See him in the garden
praying to his Father
in the deepest sorrow.

5 Yes, he is our Saviour.
Jesus died to save us,
and he rose at Easter.

6 Hallelujah
in the heav'nly Kingdom
with our living Saviour!
(. . . amen, amen.)

Traditional, altd.

85

BABEL 76.85

SVEN-ERIK BÄCK
in *71 Psalmer och Visor*, 1971

Babel

1 See them building Babel's tower:
slaves the stones are carrying.
Here no man cares for brother man.
Kyrieleison!

2 Far astray that upward road.
Man, become a stranger,
goes hungry at his brother's board—
Kyrieleison!

3 'Brotherhood'—forgotten word
down the grassy hillside
rejected from that building lies.
Kyrieleison!

4 Men one day will find it there
and will recognize it
as keystone of God's hill and house.
Hallelujah!

5 Then their cry will rise, and we
each in his own language
shall hear of brotherhood once more.
Hallelujah!

6 Mighty wind of heaven's rule,
storming every barrier,
will blow for ever where it wills.
Hallelujah!

7 So shall Babel come to nought:
where it stood shall flourish
the harvest of God's brotherhood.
Hallelujah!

Olov Hartman,
tr. Caryl Micklem (b. 1925)
and Ruth Micklem (b. 1930)

THE BEATITUDES

Set to music by WILLIAM LLEWELLYN (b. 1925)

ORGAN INTRODUCTION
Flowing easily

NOTE: *Each bar, whether* $\frac{2}{4}$ *or* $\frac{3}{4}$ *is to have the same duration.*

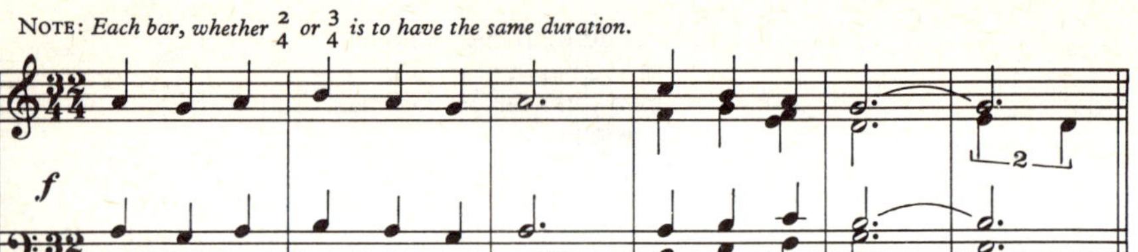

Solo
All (or Choir)
Blest are they ___ that mourn; for they shall ___ be com - for - ted.
p
(f)
Solo
All (or Choir)
Blest are ___ the meek; for they shall in - he - rit the earth.
p
(f)
ANTIPHON (sung by ALL)
f Show us your ways, ___ O Lord, teach us your paths. ___
Solo
Blest are
f
p
All (or Choir)
they that hun - ger and thirst af - ter right - eous - ness; for they shall ___ be
(f)

Solo
All (or Choir)
filled. Blest are the mer-ci-ful: for they shall ob-
p
(f)
ANTIPHON (sung by ALL)
tain mer - cy. f Show us your ways, O Lord, teach us your
f
Solo
All (or Choir)
paths. Blest are the pure in heart; for they shall
p
(f)
Solo
All (or Choir)
see God. Blest are the peace-ma-kers; for
p
(f)

Words from Psalm 25, v. 4
and Matthew 5, vv. 3-10

87

CELEBRATION 11 10. 11 10 DAVID McCARTHY (b. 1931)

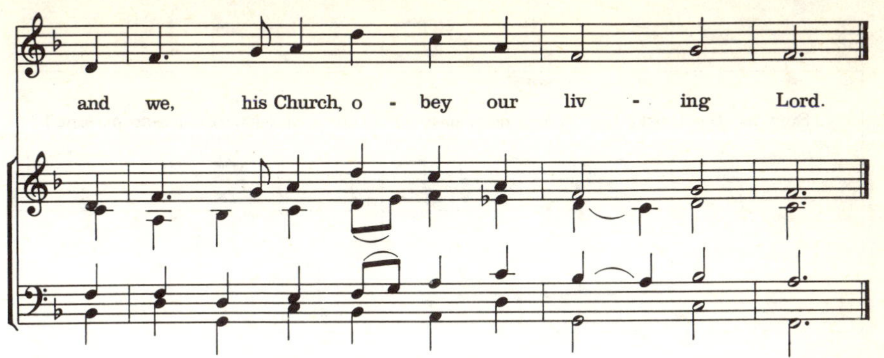

A song of celebration

1 Sing, one and all, a song of celebration,
 of love's renewal, and of hope restored,
as custom yields to ferment of creation,
 and we, his Church, obey our living Lord.

2 Rejoice that still his Spirit is descending
 with challenges that faith cannot refuse;
and ask no longer what is worth defending,
 but how to make effective God's good news.

3 We need not now take refuge in tradition,
 like men prepared to make a final stand,
but use it as a springboard of decision,
 to follow him whose Kingdom is at hand—

4 to follow him: to share his way of living;
 to shape the future as, in him, we should;
to step across the frontiers of forgiving,
 and bear the burdens of true brotherhood.

5 Creative Spirit, let your word be spoken!
 Your shock of truth invigorates the mind;
your miracles of grace shall be our token
 that only God in Christ can save mankind.

F. Pratt Green (b. 1903)

88

GOFFS OAK RICHARD H. JACQUET (b. 1947)

1 Sing to the Lord,
stars and beautiful sun,
millions of raindrops, sing!
Brooks and rivers that run,
sing to the Lord!

2 Sing to the Lord,
rolling waves on the sand,
seaweed and pebbles, sing!
Mighty mountains that stand,
sing to the Lord!

3 Sing to the Lord,
wheat that sways in the breeze,
ants ever busy, sing!
Cheerful birds in the trees,
sing to the Lord!

4 Sing to the Lord,
playful kittens and lambs,
mothers and children, sing!
Smiling babies in prams,
sing to the Lord!

5 Sing to the Lord,
great and wonderful world,
children and grown-ups, sing!
Songs of praise for this world
sing to the Lord!

Marie Odile Herve

89

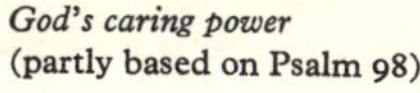

God's caring power
(partly based on Psalm 98)

ROLF SCHWEIZER

STEIN

VOICES

INSTRUMENTAL PART

Introduction, Melodic instrument

KEYBOARD

Introduction Accompaniment (ad lib)

REFRAIN
Unison
Sing to the Lord a new song, for he does won - ders.
1 – 4
VERSES
1 God
2 You
3 –
4 You
Sing to the Lord a new song, for he does won - ders.
1-4
1 – 4
Last time
Fine
won - ders.
1 tri - umphs for he is right - eous,
2 think God is the Un - known One,
3 Of - ten you don't know his pur - pose,
4 must learn to see him on - ly
Last time
Fine
Last time
Fine

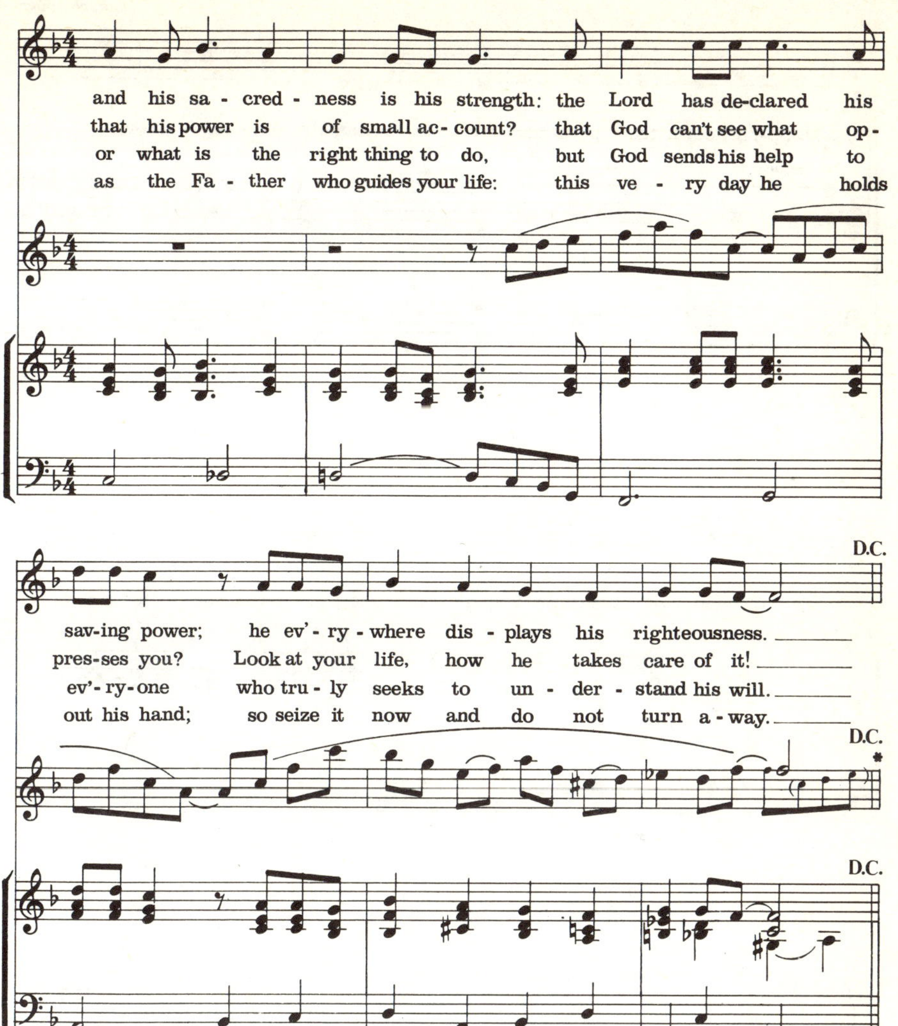

* Play the connecting notes only if the Introduction is used before each verse.

Paulus Stein
tr. F. Pratt Green (b. 1903)

PATTERNS 75.77.D.

YVONNE GOODING
and compilers

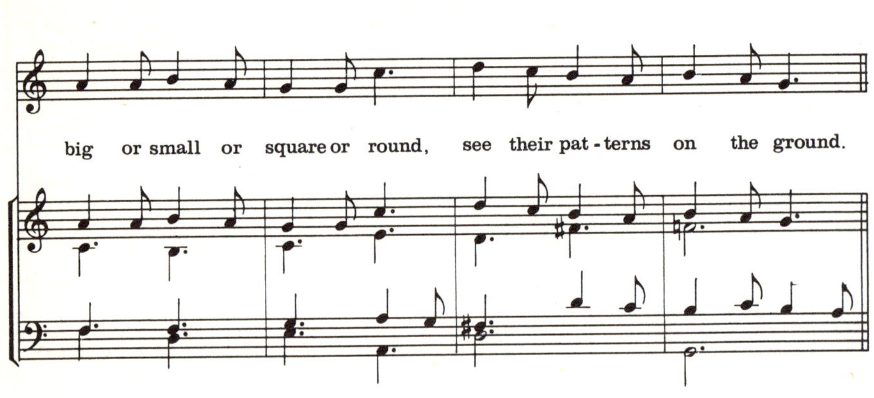

Patterns

1 Skipping down the pavement wide,
   count the paving stones;
big or small or square or round,
   see their patterns on the ground.
House and factory, church and shop,
   bricks and stones reach high.
Busy workmen made them all:
   see their patterns on the wall.

2 Look above the rooftops tall,
   far as you can see.
Clouds in daytime; stars at night;
   see their patterns in the sky.
People walking down the street,
   dressed in colours gay;
stripes and circles, frills and bows:
   see the patterns in their clothes.

3 Clouds and sunshine, night-time stars,
   clothes and curtains too;
stones and pavement, bricks and wall:
   see the patterns in them all.
Thank you, God, for sights to see
   round us every day:
still or moving; big or small;
   and the patterns in them all!

Donald H. Hilton (b. 1932)

91

ASKERSWELL D. L. M. — PETER CUTTS (b. 1937)

Creative love

1 Surrounded by a world of need,
by men to heal, to house and feed,
our mind is given to despair,
and hope is undermined by war.
Yet through the fabric of our time
there runs the liberating theme
of love that makes the world go round,
of love creative and profound.

2 This love is in the face of Christ,
in human life, made manifest;
its strong intent will conquer all,
it raises people when they fall.
Then help us, Lord, to understand
the good your purpose put in man,
and use, to bring your reign about,
those in the church and those without.

Fred Kaan (b. 1929)

WINTON 10 10 . 10 10 — GEORGE DYSON, (1883–1964)

Magnificat

1 Tell out, my soul, the greatness of the Lord!
Unnumbered blessings, give my spirit voice;
tender to me the promise of his word;
in God my Saviour shall my heart rejoice.

2 Tell out, my soul, the greatness of his name!
Make known his might, the deeds his arm has done;
his mercy sure, from age to age the same;
his holy name—the Lord, the Mighty One.

3 Tell out, my soul, the greatness of his might!
Powers and dominions lay their glory by;
proud hearts and stubborn wills are put to flight,
the hungry fed, the humble lifted high.

4 Tell out, my soul, the glories of his word!
Firm is his promise, and his mercy sure.
Tell out, my soul, the greatness of the Lord
to children's children and for evermore!

Timothy Dudley-Smith (b. 1926)

Alternative tune: WOODLANDS (CH III 440, CP 661, SP 299).

93

FIRST TUNE

DEANE 9 10 . 10 9

CARYL MICKLEM (b. 1925)

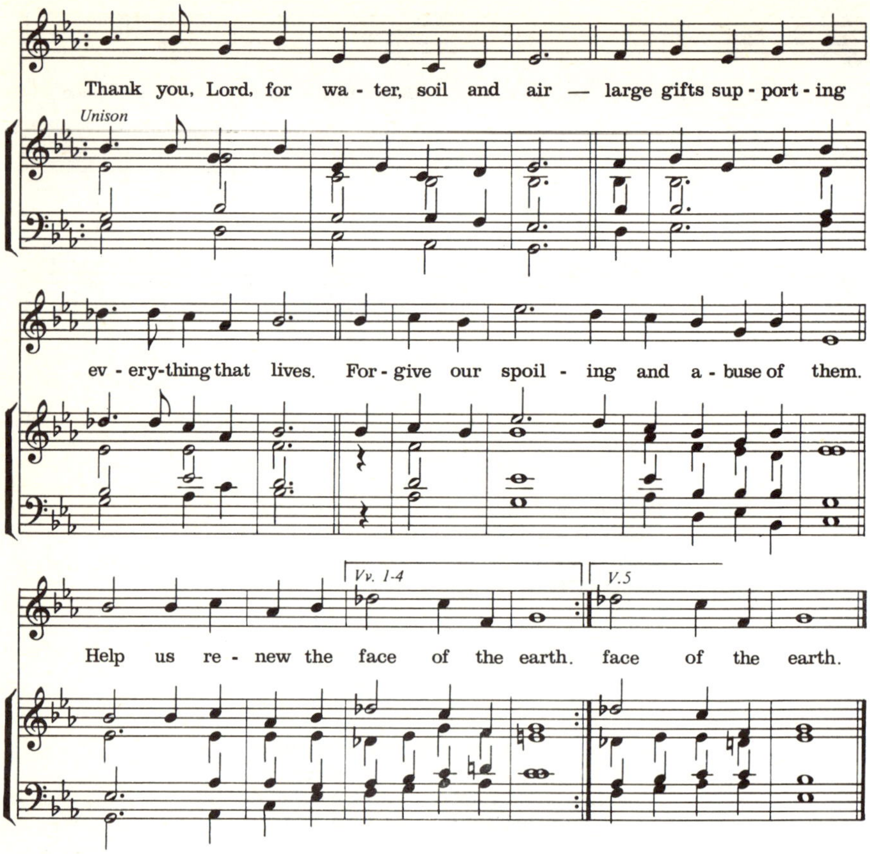
Thank you, Lord, for wa - ter, soil and air — large gifts sup - port - ing
Unison
ev - ery-thing that lives. For - give our spoil - ing and a - buse of them.
Vv. 1-4
V.5
Help us re - new the face of the earth. face of the earth.

SECOND TUNE

HOLNICOTE 9 10 . 10 9

CHARLES EDWARD STRANGE

Thank you, Lord, for wa - ter, soil and air — large gifts sup - port - ing
Unison

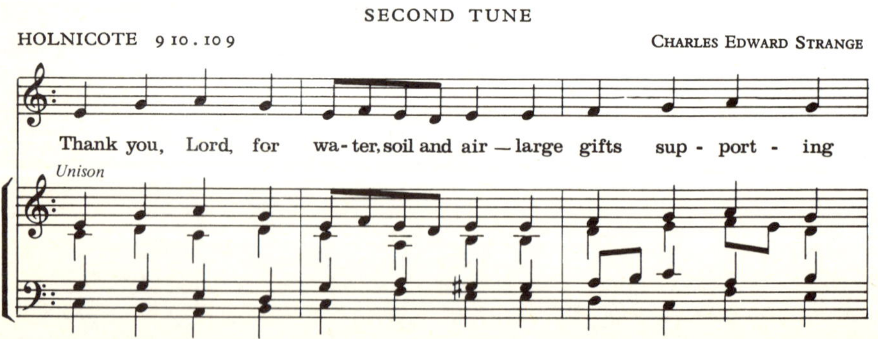

Caring for planet Earth

1 Thank you, Lord, for water, soil and air—
large gifts supporting everything that lives.
Forgive our spoiling and abuse of them.
Help us renew the face of the earth.

2 Thank you, Lord, for minerals and ores—
the basis of all building, wealth and speed.
Forgive our reckless plundering and waste.
Help us renew the face of the earth.

3 Thank you, Lord, for priceless energy—
stored in each atom, gathered from the sun.
Forgive our greed and carelessness of power.
Help us renew the face of the earth.

4 Thank you, Lord, for weaving nature's life
into a seamless robe, a fragile whole.
Forgive our haste, that tampers unawares.
Help us renew the face of the earth.

5 Thank you, Lord, for making planet Earth
a home for us and ages yet unborn.
Help us to share, consider, save and store.
Come and renew the face of the earth.

Brian Wren (b. 1936)

94

GREEN LAKE L. M. ERIK ROUTLEY (b. 1917)

The caring Church

1 The Church of Christ, in every age
 beset by change but Spirit-led,
must claim and test her heritage
 and keep on rising from the dead.

2 She has no mission but to serve,
 in proud obedience to her Lord;
to care for all, without reserve,
 to spread his liberating word.

3 Across a world, across the street,
 the victims of injustice cry
for shelter and for bread to eat,
 and never live before they die.

4 And all men suffer deeper ills:
 for there's a fever in our blood
that prostitutes our human skills
 and poisons all our brotherhood.

5 Then let the Servant Church arise,
 a caring Church that longs to be
a partner in Christ's sacrifice,
 and clothed in Christ's humanity.

6 For he alone, whose blood was shed,
 can cure the fever in our blood,
and teach us how to share our bread
 and feed the starving multitude.

F. Pratt Green (b. 1903)

Alternative tune: FUDGIE (CH III 110, NCP 17).

95

KING'S LANGLEY C. M.

Traditional May-Day carol melody, collected by Lucy Broadwood (1858–1929) and harmonised by R. Vaughan Williams (1872–1958)

1 The glory of our King was seen
   when he came riding by,
and people ran and waved and sang
   'Hosanna, King most high!'

2 The glory of our King was seen
   when, with his arms stretched wide
to show his love to everyone,
   Jesus was crucified.

3 The glory of our King was seen
   on the first Easter day,
when Christ rose up, set free from death,
   to love, to guide, to stay.

Margaret Cropper, altd.

96

ST ETHELWALD S. M. W. H. Monk (1823–89)

Lord of life and death

1 The Son of God proclaim,
the Lord of time and space;
the God who bade the light break forth
now shines in Jesus' face.

2 He, God's creative Word,
the Church's Lord and Head,
here bids us gather as his friends
and share his wine and bread.

3 The Lord of life and death
with wondering praise we sing;
we break the bread at his command
and name him God and King.

4 We take this cup in hope;
for he, who gladly bore
the shameful cross, is risen again
and reigns for evermore.

Basil E. Bridge (b. 1927)

97

BLACKBIRD LEYS 10 10 . 10 10 — PETER CUTTS (b. 1937)

Christ, the healing Word of God

1 The voice of God goes out to all the world:
his glory speaks across the universe.
The Great King's herald cries from star to star:
with power, with justice, he will walk his way.

2 The Lord has said: 'Receive my messenger,
my promise to the world, my pledge made flesh,
a lamp to every nation, light from light:
with power, with justice, he will walk his way'.

3 The broken reed he will not trample down,
nor set his heel upon the dying flame.
He binds the wounds, and health is in his hand:
with power, with justice, he will walk his way.

4 Anointed with the Spirit and with power,
he comes to crown with comfort all the weak,
to show the face of justice to the poor:
with power, with justice, he will walk his way.

5 His touch will bless the eyes that darkness held,
the lame shall run, the halting tongue shall sing,
and prisoners laugh in light and liberty:
with power, with justice, he will walk his way.

'Peter Icarus'

98

LAUDS 77.77

JOHN WILSON (b. 1905)

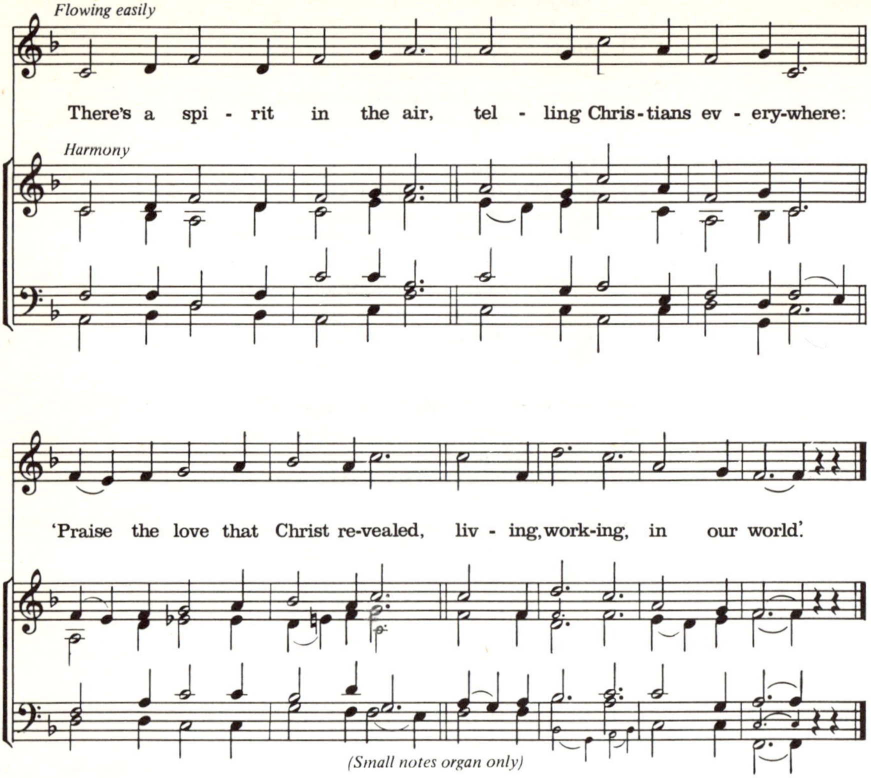

Flowing easily
There's a spi - rit in the air, tel - ling Chris-tians ev - ery-where:
Harmony
'Praise the love that Christ re-vealed, liv - ing, work-ing, in our world'.
(Small notes organ only)

(The key of F sharp may be preferred)

OPTIONAL DESCANT FOR VERSES 4 & 7

Sopranos. (Other voices sing unison melody).
Praise ___ the love! ___ Praise ___ the love! ___
Al - - - le - lu - ia! Al- - - - le - lu - ia!

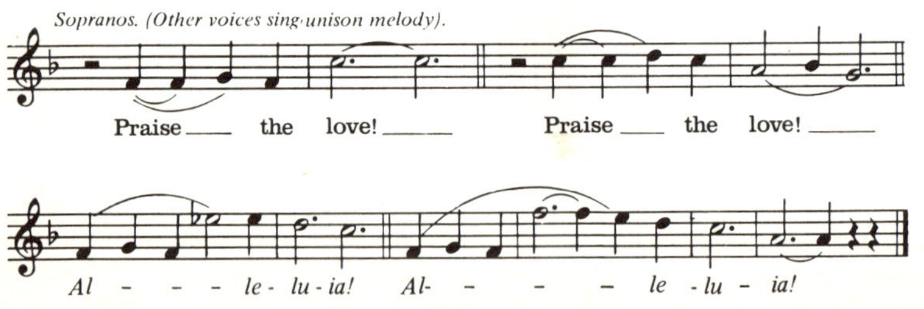

'Praise the Holy Spirit'

1 There's a spirit in the air,
telling Christians everywhere:
'Praise the love that Christ revealed,
living, working, in our world'.

2 Lose your shyness, find your tongue,
tell the world what God has done:
God in Christ has come to stay.
We can see his power today.

3 When believers break the bread,
when a hungry child is fed,
praise the love that Christ revealed,
living, working, in our world.

4 Still his Spirit leads the fight,
seeing wrong and setting right:
God in Christ has come to stay.
We can see his power today.

5 When a stranger's not alone,
where the homeless find a home,
praise the love that Christ revealed,
living, working, in our world.

6 May his Spirit fill our praise,
guide our thoughts and change our ways.
God in Christ has come to stay.
We can see his power today.

7 There's a Spirit in the air,
calling people everywhere:
praise the love that Christ revealed,
living, working, in our world.

Brian Wren (b. 1936)

99

GAUDIUM ET SPES 10 3 . 12 6 . 4 8

BRIAN WREN (b. 1936)
and compilers

This we can do

1 This we can do for justice and for peace:
  we can pray,
and work to answer prayers that other people say.
This we can do in faith
and see it through—
  for Jesus is alive today.

2 This we can do for justice and for peace:
  we can give
till every man can take life in his hands, and live.
This we can do in love
and see it through—
  for Jesus is alive today.

3 This we can do for justice and for peace:
  we can see—
and help our neighbours see—what is, and what could be.
This we can do with truth
and see it through—
  for Jesus is alive today.

4 This we can do for justice and for peace:
  we can fight
whatever hurts and tramples down, or hides the light.
This we can do with strength
and see it through—
  for Jesus is alive today.

5 This we can do for justice and for peace:
  we can hope
and, hoping, stride along our way while others grope.
This we can do till God
makes all things new—
  for Jesus is alive today.

Brian Wren (b. 1936)

100

TROTTING

ERIC REID (1936–1970)

* *Pedal notes for an organ accompaniment are shown by downward stems.*

Palm Sunday

1 Trotting, trotting through Jerusalem,
Jesus, sitting on a donkey's back,
children waving branches, singing
'Happy is he that comes in the name of the Lord!'

2 Many people in Jerusalem
thought he should have come on a mighty horse
leading all the Jews to battle—
'Happy is he that comes in the name of the Lord!'

3 Many people in Jerusalem
were amazed to see such a quiet man
trotting, trotting on a donkey—
'Happy is he that comes in the name of the Lord!'

4 Trotting, trotting through Jerusalem,
Jesus, sitting on a donkey's back:
let us join the children singing
'Happy is he that comes in the name of the Lord!'

Eric Reid (1936–1970)

101

UNISON VERSION (vv. 1 & 3)

MALHAM 88.88.88

PETER CUTTS (b. 1937)

HARMONY VERSION (v. 2)

Caryl Micklem (b. 1925)

102

FIFEHEAD 64.55.7 CARYL MICKLEM (b. 1925)

The Church taking stock of itself

1 We are your people:
Lord, by your grace,
you dare to make us
Christ to our neighbours
of every nation and race.

2 How can we demonstrate
your love and care—
speaking or listening?
battling or serving?
help us to know when and where.

3 Called to portray you,
help us to live
closer than neighbours
open to strangers,
able to clash and forgive.

4 Glad of tradition,
help us to see
in all life's changing
where you are leading,
where our best efforts should be.

5 Joined in community,
breaking your bread,
may we discover
gifts in each other,
willing to lead and be led.

6 Lord, as we minister
in different ways,
may all we're doing
show that you're living,
meeting your love with our praise.

Brian Wren (b. 1936)

103

INTERCESSOR 11 10 . 11 10 C. HUBERT H. PARRY (1848–1918)

B♮ in last verse only

The family of nations

1 We turn to you, O God of every nation,
giver of life and origin of good;
your love is at the heart of all creation,
your hurt is people's broken brotherhood.

2 We turn to you that we may be forgiven
for crucifying Christ on earth again.
We know that we have never wholly striven,
forgetting self, to love the other man.

3 Free every heart from pride and self-reliance,
our ways of thought inspire with simple grace;
break down among us barriers of defiance,
speak to the soul of all the human race.

4 Teach us, good Lord, to serve the need of others,
help us to give and not to count the cost.
Unite us all for we are born as brothers;
defeat our Babel with your Pentecost.

Fred Kaan (b. 1929)

104

PHILIPPIAN 10 10 10 . 7 CARYL MICKLEM (b. 1925)

Philippians 4.6–8

1 We praise you, Lord, for all that's true and pure—
clean lines, clear water, and an honest mind.
Grant us your truth, keep guard over our hearts,
fill all our thoughts with these things.

2 We praise you, Lord, for all that's excellent—
high mountain peaks, achievement dearly won.
Lift up our eyes, keep guard over our hearts,
fill all our thoughts with these things.

3 We praise you, Lord, for all of good report—
the spur to us of others' noble lives.
Show us your will, keep guard over our hearts,
fill all our thoughts with these things.

4 We praise you, Lord, the man of Nazareth—
you lived for others, now you live for all.
Jesus, draw near, keep guard over our hearts,
fill all our thoughts with these things.

Caryl Micklem (b. 1925)

105

LARK IN THE CLEAR AIR 96.98.D

Traditional Irish tune
arranged by compilers

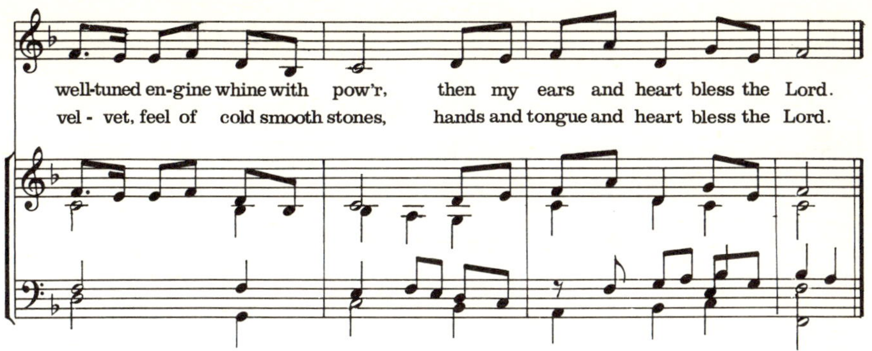

Praise with every sense

1 When I see the salmon leap the fall,
or the aer'plane's silver trail—
or a drop of water magnified,
then my eyes and heart bless the Lord.

2 When I hear the frosty crunch of snow,
or the sun-drenched hum of the bee,
or a well-tuned engine whine with power,
then my ears and heart bless the Lord.

3 When I breathe the smell of clean fresh air
blowing softly after rain,
when the strawberries are turned to jam,
then my nose and heart bless the Lord.

4 At the taste of berries gathered free,
or the tang of sea-food, mint or treacle,
touch of velvet, feel of cold smooth stones,
hands and tongue and heart bless the Lord.

Gracie King, altd.

Optional Instrumental Descant

106

ENGELBERG 10 10 10 . 4

C. V. STANFORD (1852–1924)

For a festival of praise

1 When, in man's music, God is glorified,
and adoration leaves no room for pride,
it is as though the whole creation cried
Alleluia!

2 How oft, in making music, we have found
a new dimension in the world of sound,
as worship moved us to a more profound
Alleluia!

3 So has the Church, in liturgy and song,
in faith and love, through centuries of wrong,
borne witness to the truth in every tongue.
Alleluia!

4 And did not Jesus sing a psalm that night
when utmost evil strove against the Light?
then let us sing, for whom he won the fight,
Alleluia!

5 Let every instrument be tuned for praise!
Let all rejoice who have a voice to raise!
And may God give us faith to sing always
Alleluia! Amen.

F. Pratt Green (b. 1903)

ALTERNATIVE VERSION FOR A VERSE BY THE CHOIR ALONE

107

PIOUS PRAYERS

DAVID GOODALL (b. 1922)

If the transposing link is used between verses, it is suggested that introduction and verse 1 be in B minor verse 2 in C minor, verse 3 in C♯ minor, verse 4 in D minor, with the final chord transposed up a tone.

1 When you started off the universe, Lord most high,
did you know just what would happen as years went by?
Did you in your infinite mind
everything foresee?
Or does being God mean you make a place for uncertainty?

2 When your Son allowed himself to be led away,
did he know you'd resurrect him on Easter Day?
Could he, there on Calvary's hill,
know what was to be?
Or did being yours mean he had to suffer uncertainty?

3 When your Spirit helps us all to be more complete,
seeking our co-operation and not defeat,
is it simply done for effect,
so that we'll feel free?
Or does being Spirit mean he can cope with uncertainty?

4 When we're told our faith has got to be more assured,
does it mean we ought to know all the answers, Lord?
If we had true faith in our God,
would our doubts all flee?
Or does having faith mean we thank you, Lord, for uncertainty?

John Gregory (b. 1929)

108

SWITHEN 5 6 5 . D

PETER CUTTS, (b. 1937)

1 Where is God today?
Shall we find him waiting
when we come to pray?
Will he come again
every Sunday morning?
Do we wait in vain?

2 Or can two or three,
four or five, or sixty
in his name agree,
so that we declare,
'He is here among us,
all our life to share'?

3 We have seen and heard
that which we believe in;
take him at his word.
We have seen the face
of eternal goodness,
full of truth and grace.

4 God whose face we seek
comes to life in Jesus
seventy times a week.
Every day he shows
something of his glory
to the man who knows.

5 This is how we know
that we really see him—
when like him we grow;
gain for him was loss;
for he lived for others
till he gained the cross.

6 Now the feast displays
all that he enacted;
celebrates his praise.
So once more we meet
Death and Resurrection,
and we stay—to eat.

David Goodall (b. 1922)

109

ILLSLEY L. M.

Melody, and most of the harmony,
by J. Bishop (1665–1737)

1 Your light, O God, was given to man,
  the light of truth, your wisdom's flame:
from age to age it grew more clear,
  and glorious shone when Jesus came.

2 The light of all the world was he;
  but men loved darkness more than light.
With evil deeds of pride and hate
  they scorned God's love and chose the night.

3 But light unconquered shone again;
  no cross or tomb its power could bind;
in glory, love and life arose
  to shine for ever on mankind.

4 Forgive us, Lord, if we have spurned
  your truth, your light, your wisdom's way;
and lead our hearts through Christ to find
  in love the road to perfect day.

Albert Frederick Bayly (b. 1901), *altd.*

GLORIA IN EXCELSIS

ERIK ROUTLEY (b. 1917)

*the small notes repeat the melody line and can be used for practice

glo - ry. __ Lord Je-sus Christ, on - ly Son of the Father. __ Lord God, __ Lamb of
mf
God, ______ you take a - way the sin of the world: ___ have mercy upon us; you are sea-ted at the right __ hand of the Fa - ther: ____ re - ceive our

prayer. For you a-lone are the Ho-ly one,— you a-lone are the
f
f
Lord,— you a-lone are the Most High, Je-sus Christ,— with the
Ho-ly Spi-rit in the glo-ry of God— the Fa-ther. A-men!
2
2
2
2
ff
ff

111 SANCTUS AND BENEDICTUS

ERIK ROUTLEY (b. 1917)

ACCLAMATIONS

Erik Routley (b. 1917)

ORDER OF WORSHIP
FOR
THE LORD'S SUPPER

ACKNOWLEDGEMENTS

The publishers are grateful for permission to use material as indicated below:

The text of the Authorised Version of the Bible is Crown copyright and the extract used herein is reproduced by permission.

New English Bible, second edition copyright 1970 by permission of Oxford and Cambridge University Presses.

Verses from the *Revised Standard Version of the Bible*, copyrighted 1946 and 1952 by the Division of Christian Education of the National Council of the Churches of Christ in the USA.

Texts prepared by the International Consultation on English Texts (Texts of Gloria in Excelsis, Sursum Corda, Sanctus and Benedictus) published in *Prayers we have in common* (Geoffrey Chapman 1971).

The Lord's Prayer based on the version prepared by the International Consultation on English Texts, revised and printed in Series 3 Order for Holy Communion.

The paragraph 'We thank you that Jesus was born' from *Contemporary Prayers for Public Worship*, edited by Caryl Micklem, published by SCM Press Ltd.

ORDER OF WORSHIP FOR THE LORD'S SUPPER

THE WORD AND THE PRAYERS

The Bible may be brought into the church, all standing; and the minister enters and may call the people to worship saying,

Let us worship God.

Scripture Sentences (*all standing*)

Minister This is the day which the Lord has made;
People let us rejoice and be glad in it.
Minister It is good to give thanks to the Lord;
People for his love endures for ever.

Other sentences may be used or seasonal sentences added.

Prayer of Approach

Minister Let us pray.

Almighty God,
to whom all hearts are open,
all desires known,
and from whom no secrets are hid:
cleanse the thoughts of our hearts
by the inspiration of your Holy Spirit,
that we may perfectly love you,
and worthily magnify your holy Name;
through Christ our Lord. **Amen.**

Or this prayer may be used:

Almighty God, infinite and eternal
in wisdom, power and love:
we praise you for all that you are,
and for all that you do for the world.
You have shown us your truth and your love
in our Saviour Jesus Christ.
Help us by your Spirit
to worship you in spirit and in truth;
through Jesus Christ our Lord. **Amen.**

Hymn or Psalm

Confession of Sin (*all kneel or sit*)

Minister Let us confess our sins to God
and ask his forgiveness.

All	**Lord God most merciful,** **we confess that we have sinned,** **through our own fault,** **and in common with others,** **in thought, word and deed,** **and through what we have left undone.** **We ask to be forgiven.** **By the power of your Spirit** **turn us from evil to good,** **help us to forgive others,** **and keep us in your ways** **of righteousness and love;** **through Jesus Christ our Lord. Amen.**

Assurance of Pardon

Minister	In repentance and in faith receive the promise of grace and the assurance of pardon: Here are words you may trust, words that merit full acceptance: 'Christ Jesus came into the world to save sinners.' Your sins are forgiven for his sake.
People	**Thanks be to God.**

Or this Assurance may be used:

Minister	God so loved the world that he gave his only Son, that whoever believes in him should not perish but have eternal life. To all who repent and believe, we declare, in the name of the Father, the Son and the Holy Spirit: God grants you the forgiveness of your sins.
People	**Thanks be to God.**

The Kyries (*may be said*)

Minister	Lord, have mercy on us.
People	**Christ, have mercy on us.** **Lord, have mercy on us.**

Gloria in excelsis *(all standing)*

All **Glory to God in the highest,**
and peace to his people on earth.

Lord God, heavenly King,
almighty God and Father,
we worship you, we give you thanks,
we praise you for your glory.

Lord Jesus Christ, only Son of the Father,
Lord God, Lamb of God,
you take away the sin of the world:
have mercy on us;
you are seated at the right hand of the Father:
receive our prayer.

For you alone are the Holy One,
you alone are the Lord,
you alone are the Most High,
Jesus Christ, with the Holy Spirit,
in the glory of God the Father. Amen.

Prayer for Grace

The collect of the day or other prayer for grace may be said here or after the sermon.

The Minister may then introduce the theme of the day's service, and may speak in particular to the children, and a hymn may be sung before the children leave; or the minister may speak to the children after one of the readings.

Old Testament Reading

and/or a New Testament Reading

Psalm, Canticle, Hymn or Anthem

New Testament Reading

or readings: Epistle and Gospel

A hymn may be sung.

Sermon

The sermon may be followed by a silence and/or a prayer.

Hymn

The notices may be given here or after the prayers.

Prayers for the Church and the World

After each paragraph a versicle and response may be said, such as

V. Lord, in your mercy,
R. Hear our prayer.

The special subjects after the words 'We pray for' are merely suggestions; others may be substituted; omissions may be made. Intervals of silence should be kept.
The paragraphs may be used as a continuous prayer by the omission of the words 'We pray for' and the words in italics.

Minister Let us pray.

Almighty God,
whose Spirit helps us in our weakness
and guides us in our prayers;
we pray for the Church and for the world
in the name of Jesus Christ.

We pray for

the Church throughout the world
our ministers, elders and members
local unity and witness

Renew the faith and life of the Church;
strengthen its witness;
and make it one in Christ.
Grant that we
and all who confess that he is Lord
may be faithful in service
and filled with his spirit,
and that the world may be turned to him.

We pray for

the nations of the world
our own country
all who work for reconciliation

Guide the nations
in the ways of justice, liberty and peace;
and help them to seek
the unity and welfare of mankind.
Give to our Queen and to all in authority
wisdom to know and strength to do
what is right.

We pray for

those in trade and industry
members of the professions
all who serve the community

Grant that men and women in their various callings
may have grace to do their work well;
and may the resources of the earth be wisely used,
truth honoured and preserved,
and the quality of our life enriched.

We pray for

the sick and the suffering
victims of injustice
the lonely and the bereaved

Comfort those in sorrow;
heal the sick in body or in mind;
and deliver the oppressed.
Give us active sympathy
for all who suffer; and help us
so to bear the burdens of others
that we may fulfil the law of Christ.

We pray for

our families
friends and neighbours
all who need our prayers

Keep us and the members of our families
united in loyalty and in love,
and always in your care;
and may our friends and neighbours,
and all for whom we pray,
receive the help they need,
and live in peace.

We remember those who have died

Eternal God, accept our thanks and praise
for all who have served you faithfully here on earth,
and especially for those dear to our own hearts . . .
May we and all your people,
past, present and to come,
share the life and joy of your kingdom;
through Jesus Christ our Lord. **Amen.**

The notices, if not already given, may be given here.

The Invitation and the Gracious Words

The minister may then give an invitation to those present, to whatever branch of the Church they belong, to share in the Lord's Supper.

Minister Hear the gracious words of
our Lord Jesus Christ;

Come to me,
all who labour and are heavy-laden,
and I will give you rest.

I am the bread of life;
he who comes to me shall not hunger,
and he who believes in me shall never thirst.

Him who comes to me
I will not cast out.

The Peace

Minister The peace of the Lord Jesus Christ
be with you all.
People **Peace be with you.**

Offertory

The offerings of the people are collected.

All stand when the offerings are brought to the Table.

The bread and wine may be carried into the church and brought to the Table; or, if they have been prepared on the Table before the service begins, the bread and wine are uncovered.

Then a prayer is said, all standing.

Minister Let us pray.

All **Eternal God,**
we come with these gifts
to offer our sacrifice of praise
and the service of our lives;
through Jesus Christ our Lord. Amen.

Hymn

This hymn may be sung while the money, bread and wine are brought to the Table, in which case the offertory prayer follows the hymn.

The Narrative of the Institution of the Lord's Supper (1 Corinthians 11 : 23–26)

Minister
Hear the narrative of the institution
of the Lord's Supper as it was recorded
by the apostle Paul.

I received from the Lord what I also delivered
to you, that the Lord Jesus
on the night when he was betrayed
took bread, and when he had given thanks,
he broke it, and said,
'This is my body which is for you.
Do this in remembrance of me.'
In the same way also
the cup, after supper, saying,
'This cup is the new covenant in my blood.
Do this, as often as you drink it,
in remembrance of me.'
For as often as you eat this bread
and drink the cup, you proclaim the Lord's death
until he comes.

The Taking of the Bread and Wine

Minister
In the name of the Lord Jesus Christ,
and following his example,
we take this bread and this cup,
and give thanks to God.

The Thanksgiving (*all standing*)

Minister Lift up your hearts.
People We lift them to the Lord.
Minister Let us give thanks to the Lord our God.
People It is right to give him thanks and praise.
Minister With joy we give you thanks and praise,
Almighty God, Source of all life and love,
that we live in your world,
that you are always
creating and sustaining it by your power,
and that you have so made us
that we can know and love you,
trust and serve you.

We give you thanks
that you loved the world so much
that you gave your only Son,
so that everyone who has faith in him
may not die but have eternal life.

Here may follow a seasonal or other special thanksgiving; or else the prayer continues:

We thank you that Jesus was born among us;
that he lived our common life on earth;
that he suffered and died for us;
that he rose again;
and that he is always present
through the Holy Spirit.

We thank you that we can live in the faith
that your kingdom will come,
and that in life, in death
and beyond death you are with us.

Then, or after the special thanksgiving, the prayer continues:

Therefore with all the company of heaven,
and with all your people,
of all places and times,
we proclaim your greatness and sing your praise.

All **Holy, holy, holy Lord**
God of power and might,
Heaven and earth are full of your glory.
Hosanna in the highest.

Minister Blessed is he
who comes in the name of the Lord.

All **Hosanna in the highest.**

Minister Holy Lord God,
by what we do here
in remembrance of Christ
we celebrate
his perfect sacrifice on the Cross
and his glorious resurrection and ascension;
we declare
that he is Lord of all;
and we prepare for
his coming in his kingdom.

We pray that
through your Holy Spirit
this bread may be for us
the body of Christ
and this wine
the blood of Christ.

Accept our sacrifice of praise;
and as we eat and drink
at his command
unite us to Christ
as one body in him,
and give us strength
to serve you in the world.

And to you,
one holy and eternal God,
Father, Son and Holy Spirit,
we give praise and glory,
now and for ever. **Amen.**

The Lord's Prayer

Minister And now, as our Saviour Christ
has taught us, we say,

All **Our Father in heaven,**
hallowed be your Name,
your kingdom come,
your will be done,
on earth as in heaven.
Give us today our daily bread.
Forgive us our sins
as we forgive those who sin against us.
Do not bring us to the time of trial
but deliver us from evil.
For the kingdom, the power, and the glory are yours
now and for ever. Amen.

The Breaking of the Bread *(all sit)*

Minister The Lord Jesus
on the night when he was betrayed
took bread (*here the minister takes the bread in his hands*), and when he had given thanks,
he broke it (*here the minister breaks the bread*), and said,
'This is my body which is for you.
Do this in remembrance of me.'

In the same way also the cup (*here the minister raises the cup*), saying,
'This cup is the new convenant in my blood.
Do this, as often as you drink it,
in remembrance of me.'

Or, if the narrative of the institution has been used earlier in the service, as he breaks the bread the minister may say:

The bread which we break
is the communion of the body of Christ.

And as he raises the cup he may say:

The cup of blessing which we bless
is the communion of the blood of Christ.

The Sharing of the Bread and Wine

In giving the bread the minister says:

Take, eat; this is the body of Christ
which is broken for you;
do this in remembrance of him.

or,

The body of our Lord Jesus Christ,
given for you.

In giving the cup the minister says:

This cup is the new covenant
in the blood of Christ,
shed for you and for many
for the remission of sins:
drink of it.

or,

The blood of our Lord Jesus Christ,
shed for you.

Acclamation *(may be said or sung)*

Minister Let us praise the Lord.

All **Christ has died.**
Christ is risen.
In Christ shall all be made alive.

Blessing and honour and glory and power be to our God for ever and ever. Amen.

Prayer after Communion

Minister Let us pray.

Most gracious God,
we praise you
for what you have given
and for what you have promised us here.

You have made us one
with all your people
in heaven and on earth.
You have fed us
with the bread of life,
and renewed us for your service.

Now we give ourselves to you;
and we ask
that our daily living
may be part of the life of your kingdom,

and that our love
may be your love reaching out into the life of the world;
through Jesus Christ our Lord. **Amen.**

Hymn or Doxology

Dismissal and Blessing

Minister Go in peace to serve the Lord;
and the blessing of God Almighty,
the Father, the Son and the Holy Spirit,
be with you always. **Amen.**

ALPHABETICAL INDEX OF TUNES

METRICAL INDEX OF TUNES

INDEX OF COMPOSERS, ARRANGERS AND SOURCES OF TUNES

A number in italics indicates a Harmonization, Arrangement, or Descant

---

INDEX OF AUTHORS, TRANSLATORS AND SOURCES OF WORDS

A number in italics indicates a Translation

SUBJECT INDEX

The index is in three sections: *The Christian Year*, *Worship* (*including Sacraments and Special Occasions*) and *Worship Themes.*

Entries in italics are to be found in the Order of Worship for the Lord's Supper.

THE CHRISTIAN YEAR

WORSHIP (INCLUDING SACRAMENTS AND SPECIAL OCCASIONS)

WORSHIP THEMES

INDEX OF FIRST LINES